Grades **K-2**

Scott Foresman

Comprehension
Teacher's Guide and Student Worktext

Glenview, Illinois
Boston, Massachusetts
Chandler, Arizona
Upper Saddle River, New Jersey

ISBN-13: 978-0-328-47834-7
ISBN-10:   0-328-47834-2
9 10 V016 18 17 16 15 14 13

Reading Street Intervention Kit

Program Overview

The *Reading Street Response to Intervention Kit* provides targeted instruction in core English-Language Arts standards for Grades K to 2 in each of the five critical areas of reading instruction: phonemic awareness, phonics and decoding, fluency, vocabulary, and comprehension. The Kit, designed for small-group or one-on-one instruction, includes lessons on core skills, allowing teachers to focus on the skills children need most and to help children make rapid progress to achieve grade-level proficiency.

Each lesson includes three customized mini-lessons differentiated for the following reading and skill levels:

Mini-lesson 1: Level 1 (pre-K to K)
Mini-lesson 2: Level 2 (K to Grade 1)
Mini-lesson 3: Level 3 (Grades 1 to 2)

For additional information about the *Reading Street Response to Intervention Kit*, see "How to Use This Kit" in the Placement Tests book on pp. T•4–T•6.

Comprehension Teacher's Guide and Student Worktext

The Teacher's Guide portion includes

- three-tiered, differentiated lessons for 15 core skills and strategies
- lessons on how to approach nonfiction and fiction
- reinforcement for the strategies and routines used in the core program

The Student Worktext portion includes

- additional reading opportunities
- additional skills practice
- graphic organizers
- School+Home activities

Lesson Features

- **Set the scene** introduces the lesson topic to children.
- **Objectives** identify the instructional objectives for children.
- **Materials** list the Student Worktext components and additional supporting materials for the lesson, such as the Leveled Reader Database.
- **Direct teaching** is provided through explicit teacher modeling and consistent routines.
- **Model passages** allow teachers to model the skill or strategy.
- **Mini-lessons** allow for differentiated instruction.
- **Guided practice** for each mini-lesson consists of ample group practice with multiple response opportunities.
- **Independent practice (On Their Own)** allows children to read and apply skills independently or with teacher guidance.
- **If…/then…** provides teachers with specific activities for reinforcing skills.

Table of Contents Comprehension

Comprehension
Teacher's Guide

How to Approach Fiction

Tell children that fiction tells a story about made-up characters and events. Story structure is the arrangement of a story. Explain that fiction always has characters, a setting, a theme, and a plot.

Use the checklist below to explain to children that there are many strategies good readers use before, during, and after reading. For further instruction on teaching and applying these strategies, see the RTI Kit Implementation Guide.

BEFORE READING STRATEGIES

❏ **Activate Background Knowledge** Background knowledge – information readers already know about a topic based on their reading and personal experience – allows children to make connections to people, places, and things from the real world.

❏ **Predict and Set Purpose** By predicting and setting a purpose for reading, struggling readers further connect themselves to text by personalizing their interaction with it.

DURING READING STRATEGIES

❏ **Question** Explain to children that asking questions before, during, and after reading is an important tool for reading any type of text.

❏ **Monitor and Clarify Comprehension** When monitoring their comprehension, children should determine not only *what* they don't understand, but also *why* they don't understand.

❏ **Visualize** Tell children that when they visualize, they collaborate with an author by taking the author's words and making them their own by creating pictures in their mind.

❏ **Code Text** Coding text helps struggling readers monitor their comprehension and remember what they've read.

❏ **Use Graphic Organizers** Completing graphic organizers while they read helps struggling readers organize, understand, and remember information both as they read and after reading.

AFTER READING STRATEGIES

❏ **Retell** Remind struggling readers to include only main events and to think about the characters, the setting, and the plot as they retell.

❏ **Reflect** To better understand the way they approach and navigate fiction, children should ask themselves questions, such as, "What features of the story's structure helped me understand the story?"

How to Approach Expository Text

Tell children that expository text tells about real people, places, or things. It can be organized by cause and effect, problem and solution, question and answer, comparison and contrast, description, and sequence.

Use the checklist below to explain to children that there are many strategies good readers use before, during, and after reading. For further instruction on teaching and applying these strategies, see the RTI Kit Implementation Guide.

BEFORE READING STRATEGIES

❐ **Activate Prior Knowledge**   Background knowledge allows children to connect to the text.

❐ **Build Background Knowledge**   To build background knowledge, readers can stop and explain a text-to-self connection that arises in their thinking.

❐ **Set a Purpose for Reading**   Keep struggling readers focused and motivated by clearly establishing a purpose with children.

❐ **Overview the Text**   Focus overviewing, a form of skimming and scanning the text before reading, on features such as text structure.

DURING READING STRATEGIES

❐ **Question**   Asking questions before, during, and after reading helps children evaluate their understanding.

❐ **Determine Important Ideas**   To identify important ideas, children can refer to the expository features and structures, such as headings.

❐ **Monitor and Clarify Comprehension**   Use background knowledge and strategies such as asking questions to clarify understanding.

❐ **Draw Inferences**   Children can infer ideas about what the author is trying to present by combining what they already know with text clues.

❐ **Synthesize Information**   Readers can reach new insights that change the way they think by reviewing, sorting, and sifting information.

❐ **Visualize**   When struggling readers get pictures in their mind while reading, they are more likely to keep reading.

❐ **Code Text**   Coding text helps struggling readers monitor their comprehension and remember what they've read.

❐ **Use Graphic Organizers**   Visual displays of key ideas help struggling readers categorize content and pull important ideas from text.

❐ **Understand New Vocabulary**   Reading on, rereading, and reading surrounding sentences helps determine the meaning of new words.

AFTER READING STRATEGIES

❐ **Summarize**   Tell struggling readers to include only main ideas as they summarize.

❐ **Reflect**   Children should ask themselves questions, such as, "What features helped me understand the text?"

Comprehension Lesson 1
Author's Purpose

Objectives:
- Identify the author.
- Identify the author's purpose for writing.
- Distinguish four purposes for writing.

MATERIALS
Worktext pp. 2–7
T-Chart, p. 100
Web, p. 102
Leveled Reader Database

Set the scene When someone writes a story, that person is an author. Authors write for a reason, or purpose. For example, they might write to share a funny story to make readers laugh. Or they might write to explain something important to readers. When you know an author's purpose for writing, you understand what the writing is about and how you should read it.

Model Read aloud "The Hot Day."

The Hot Day
The summer day was too hot. Ken jumped into the cool water. It felt great.
"I am not coming out of the water until it's time to start school!" Ken yelled. Ken's mother shook her head and smiled.

There are several purposes, or reasons, for writing. **Tell children you will write them in a T-Chart (from p. 100). Write:** *Inform, Entertain, Describe,* and *Convince* in the left column. After giving each explanation that follows, write it in the right column, in the appropriate row. When authors write to *inform,* they give the reader important information. Authors write to *entertain* when they want to tell an interesting or entertaining story. When authors write to *describe* something, they write about how it looks, sounds, feels, tastes, and smells. When authors write to *convince,* they try to make the reader think or act in a certain way.

Reread "The Hot Day." I can decide what reason the author had for writing. The passage does not give important information. It does not describe anything or tell me to think or act in a certain way. I think the author wrote the passage to entertain me.

Remind children that...
- an author is the person who writes a text.
- authors write for a reason, such as to inform, to entertain, to describe, and to convince.

Guide Practice
Read the following story aloud.

The Missing Lunch
by Sara Lopez

The bell rang for lunch. At last! Sal was hungry. He looked for his lunch. He could not find it. He looked and looked. All of the other children went to eat. Sal went, but he did not have his lunch.

"Sal!" called Ben. Ben was Sal's brother. "There you are!" Ben put a paper bag on the table. "I have your lunch!" Who is the author? *(Sara Lopez)* What is her reason for writing the story? *(to entertain)*

If... children have trouble identifying the author's reason for writing,

then... point out that the passage is a story. Most stories are written to entertain readers.

On Their Own As children read "Before the Storm" on Worktext p. 2 independently or with you, have them use the T-Chart on p. 100 to identify the author of each passage and the author's reason for writing. For additional practice, assign p. 3.

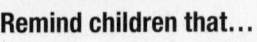

Mini-Lesson 2

Remind children that...
- authors have reasons for writing.
- there are four main purposes, or reasons, authors write: to entertain, to inform, to describe, and to convince.

Guide Practice
Then read aloud the following paragraph.

Hold the toothbrush in your mouth. Move the toothbrush back and forth. Brush the front and back of each tooth, top and bottom. Brush until your mouth is clean.

What is the author's reason for writing this paragraph? Have children agree that the reason is to inform readers of how to brush their teeth. How did you decide this? Help children understand that the paragraph gives important information about the topic of brushing teeth.

If... children have trouble understanding the author's reason for writing,

then... read the first sentence and explain that it tells readers how to do something (holding a toothbrush in your mouth). Review each sentence to show that the purpose of the text is to inform.

On Their Own As children read the letter on Worktext p. 4 independently or with you, have them use the T-Chart on p. 100 with the four author's purposes listed as they read. For additional practice, assign p. 5.

Mini-Lesson 3

Remind children that...
- there are four main purposes, or reasons, for writing: to inform, to entertain, to describe, and to convince.
- knowing the author's purpose helps readers understand what they read.

Guide Practice
Read aloud "The Biggest Signs."

The Biggest Signs

We have all seen huge signs that show things to buy. Large signs like these are called *billboards*. People made the first billboards more than 100 years ago. The first billboards were circus signs. Soon many companies started using billboards.

The author's purpose here is to *inform* because the text gives information about a topic: the history of billboards. Create a Web. Place *information about billboards* in the

center. Now that I know the author's purpose, I can use that information to understand the text. The text says that billboards are more than 100 years old. Write this in an outer circle. Continue with other facts.

If... children have difficulty remembering the text,
then... reread it one sentence at a time so they can fill in the Web.

On Their Own As children read "Knut, the Famous Polar Bear" on Worktext p. 6 independently or with you, have them use the Web to determine the author's purpose and information about the topic. For additional practice, assign p. 7.

Cause and Effect

Objectives:
- Identify cause and effect.
- Recognize cause-effect relationships.
- Identify cause-effect signal words.

MATERIALS

Worktext pp. 8–13
Cause and Effect Organizer, p. 92
Leveled Reader Database

Set the scene Tell children that most things in a story happen for a reason. A *cause* is something that happens. An *effect* is the reason it happens. We can understand a story better by asking ourselves *What happens?* and *Why does it happen?* Clue words such as *so, because,* and *since* help us figure out what happens and why.

Model Read aloud "Bella and Tarra." Ask children to listen closely to identify the causes and effects.

Tarra and Bella

Circus and zoo elephants can get very old or sick, <u>so</u> many of them move to a special park in Tennessee that takes care of elephants. <u>Because</u> elephants like to live in pairs, they quickly look for a best friend. One elephant found a friend that surprised everyone. Tarra became best friends with Bella. People were surprised <u>because</u> Bella is a stray dog. <u>Since</u> they're best friends, Tarra and Bella do everything together. They eat, sleep, and play together.

Tell children you will use a Cause and Effect Organizer (from p. 92) to keep track of what happens and why those things happen. I'm going to read the story again and look for clue words. **Reread the first sentence.** *So* is a clue word. I will ask myself *What happens?* This sentence tells me that elephants move to a park in Tennessee that takes care of them. I will write that in the bottom oval.

Next, I will ask myself *Why does it happen?* The sentence says that elephants get very old or sick. **Have children help you find cause-and-effect relationships in the other sentences.**

Remind children that...
- an effect is what happens.
- a cause is why that thing happens.

Guide Practice

Help children understand cause-and-effect relationships by giving them everyday examples, such as waking up when the alarm rings or tripping if your shoes are untied.

Ask children to help you find the cause-and-effect relationships in other sentences. *We forgot our umbrella, so we got wet in the rain.* What happens? (We got wet in the rain.) Why does it happen? (We forgot our umbrella.) As a group, work together to write what happens and why it happens.

Repeat the procedure with these sentences.

- *Maria baked a cake because it was her mom's birthday.* What happens? (Maria baked a cake.) Why does it happen? (It was her mom's birthday.)
- *The heater broke, so the classroom was cold.* What happens? (The classroom was cold.) Why does it happen? (The heater broke.)

If... children have trouble identifying cause and effect, **then...** act out cause-effect relationships, such as darkening the room by turning off the lights and have children answer the questions *What happens?* and *Why does it happen?*

On Their Own As children read "Closed!" on Worktext p. 8 independently or with you, have them complete a Cause and Effect Organizer from p. 92 to help them identify causes and effects. For additional practice, assign p. 9.

Mini-Lesson 2

Remind children that...
- causes always happen first.
- an effect is the result of the cause.
- words such as *because, since,* and *so* signal cause-effect relationships.

Guide Practice
Have children look for signal words to identify cause-effect relationships in the sentences below. Point out that a cause, or why something happens, appears after the word *because.* An effect, or what happens, appears after the word *so. Lou forgot to close the hamster cage, so his hamster got loose.* What is the clue word? (*so*) What happens? (Lou's hamster got loose.) Why does it happen? (He didn't close the cage.)

Then read aloud the following paragraph, using the same procedure.

Mia Hamm started playing soccer when she was about 12 years old. Because she was so good, Mia made the U.S. National Team at a very young age. Mia scored lots of goals and won Olympic medals in her career, so she is one of the world's most famous soccer players.

What clue words to you see? (*because, so*) What's one thing that happened? (Mia made the U.S. National Team at a young age.) Why did it happen? (She played very well.)

If... children have trouble identifying cause-effect relationships,
then... focus on identifying signal words first.

On Their Own Have children read "Thank You, Busy Bees" on Worktext p. 10, independently or with you, filling out the Cause and Effect Organizer on p. 92 as they read. For additional practice, assign p. 11.

Mini-Lesson 3

Remind children that...
- words such as *since, because,* and *so* signal cause and effect.
- sometimes a cause triggers multiple effects.

Guide Practice
Help children understand words that signal cause-effect relationships. *Since we were late to the movie, we missed the previews.* What is the clue word? (*since*) What happens? (They missed the previews.) Why does it happen? (They were late.)

Point out that sometimes there may be more than one effect. What things does a bad storm cause? (A bad storm can cause fallen trees, damaged homes, and blackouts). Point out that the multiple effects have a single cause (the storm).

Read aloud the paragraph. Since Annie got a camera for her birthday, she began taking pictures of everything. She took pictures of her parents and little brother at the park. Annie also took a funny picture of her cat chasing a fuzzy ball.

What clue word to you see? (*since*) What things happened? (Annie took pictures of her family. She took pictures of her cat.) Why did these things happen? (Annie got a camera for her birthday.)

If... children have trouble identifying cause and effect,
then... display cause-effect sentences on the board, circle the signal words, and draw arrows from the cause to the effect.

On Their Own Have children read "A Soggy Lunch" on Worktext p. 12 independently or with you, using the Cause and Effect Organizer from p. 92. For additional practice, assign p. 13.

Compare and Contrast

Objectives:
- Identify how things are alike and different.
- Recognize comparison-contrast relationships.
- Identify compare and contrast clue words.

MATERIALS

Worktext pp. 14–19
T-Chart, p. 100
Leveled Reader Database

Set the scene When you compare and contrast, you tell how two or more things are alike or different. *Alike* means how things are the same. *Different* means how things are not the same. Clue words such as *like, similarly, unlike,* and *however* show how things are alike or different.

Model Read aloud "Kate's Big Day" and "Amy's Horrible Morning."

Kate's Big Day

Kate woke up early. She had to turn in a paper in class. Her paper was on swimming. That was the sport she liked best. Kate finished her paper last night. She wanted to do well on it. Kate picked up the paper from her desk and placed it in her bag. Then she had breakfast and walked to school.

Amy's Horrible Morning

Amy woke up late. Oh, no! She wanted to wake up early. She had to finish her paper. She wanted to do well on it. Her paper was on soccer. That was the sport she liked best. Amy picked up her paper from the floor and threw it into her bag. She ran to catch the bus.

Use a T-Chart to record likenesses and differences in the stories. Label the column heads *Alike* and *Different*. First, I can write in the *Alike* column that both stories are about girls writing papers. Next, I can write in the *Different* column that Kate finished her paper, but Amy didn't finish her paper. **Continue modeling, adding more likenesses and differences to the chart.**

Mini-Lesson 1

Remind children that...
- *alike* (compare) means telling how things are the same.
- *different* (contrast) means telling how things are not the same.

Guide Practice
Remind children that they tell how things are alike and different every day. Give real-world examples, such as comparing and contrasting to decide which product to buy at a store or which movie to see.

Ask children to help you complete the chart by identifying other ways how else the stories about Kate and Amy are alike and different. How else are Kate and Amy alike? How are they different? For example, under *Alike* we can put that both Kate and Amy like sports. Write *like sports* under *Alike. Different:* Kate's favorite sport is swimming, but Amy's is soccer. Add these details to the chart. As a group, work together to find as many likenesses and differences between the two stories as possible.

If... children have trouble finding likenesses and differences,

then... ask them more specific compare-contrast questions, such as How do Kate and Amy get to school? After children respond, repeat their answers using compare-contrast clue words, such as *Kate walks to school,* but *Amy rides the bus.*

On Their Own As children read "Kim's New School" and "Joe's New School" on Worktext p. 14 independently or with you, have them complete a T-Chart from p. 100. For additional practice, assign p. 15.

Mini-Lesson 2

Remind children that...
- comparisons, or likenesses, tell how things are the same.
- contrasts, or differences, tell how things are different.

Guide Practice

Finding likenesses and differences helps readers better understand and remember what they read. Children can double-check likenesses and differences they find by rereading the text.

Write this paragraph on the board. Then read it aloud to children.

> Tom and Eric both wanted a dog. Tom's parents let him get a dog. He picked a dog named Blue. But Eric's parents thought dogs were too much work. They let Eric get a cat instead. Eric picked a cat also named Blue.

Ask children the following questions:
- How are the characters alike and different?
- How are the pets alike and different?
- How are the events in the boys' lives similar and different?

After they answer each question, have children circle parts of the paragraph that helped them find likenesses and differences.

If... children have trouble identifying likenesses and differences,

then... reread the paragraph and circle the words and phrases indicating likenesses or differences.

On Their Own As children read "Hiking Trip" and "A Walk at Night" on Worktext p. 16 independently or with you, have them complete a T-Chart from p. 100. For additional practice, assign p. 17.

Mini-Lesson 3

Remind children that...
- comparing tells how things are alike.
- contrasting tells how things are different.

Guide Practice

Help children understand clue words that signal compare and contrast. Words such as *like, both,* and *similarly* signal comparison, and *unlike, but,* and *however* signal contrast. *Sara likes swimming, but Kevin likes fishing.* What is the clue word? *(but)* What is being compared or contrasted? *(what Sara and Kevin like is contrasted)*

Read the following paragraph aloud.

> Both Sara and Kevin each went on a trip last summer. Sara's family flew to Miami, but Kevin's family drove to Lake Michigan. The weather was hot during Sara's trip. However, it was cold during Kevin's trip. Like Sara, Kevin did not want to go home.

What clue words did you hear? *(both, but, however, like)* Use the clue words to identify comparisons and contrasts in the story. For each comparison or contrast they make, have children support it with evidence from the text.

If... children have trouble identifying comparisons and contrasts,

then... focus on identifying clue words first.

On Their Own As children read "Aunt Elsa" on Worktext p. 18 independently or with you, have them complete a T-Chart from p. 100. For additional practice, assign p. 19.

Comprehension Lesson 4
Main Idea and Details

Objectives:
- Identify the main idea.
- Identify supporting details.
- Distinguish main idea and details.

MATERIALS
Worktext pp. 20–25
Main Idea Organizer, p. 96
Main Idea and Supporting Details Organizer, p. 97
Leveled Reader Database

Set the scene The main idea of a passage tells what the passage is mostly about. Supporting details describe or explain the main idea. Identify the main idea and supporting details to better understand what you read.

Model Read aloud "My First Plane Ride." Ask children to listen closely so they can identify the main idea.

My First Plane Ride

I am going on my first airplane ride. I am going to see my grandmother. She lives far away. I will ride in the airplane for three hours.

I am going to take my bag. I packed it with books, pens, and paper.

My dad says that I might feel afraid. I am not afraid now. I want to see what the sky looks like from an airplane!

To help me understand this passage, I'm going to think about the main idea of the passage, or what it is mostly about. **Use the Main Idea graphic organizer to model how to identify main idea.**

What is the title of the passage? The title is "My First Plane Ride." I will write that on the organizer. I want to find out the main idea of the passage. The main idea is stated in the first sentence. I will write that on the organizer. I know this because the other sentences tell things about the person taking his or her first plane ride. I will include this information in the organizer.

Mini-Lesson 1

Remind children that...
- the main idea is what the text is mostly about.
- the main idea is the most important idea of a text.

Guide Practice
Read aloud "Little Bear."

Little Bear

Judy has a new puppy. She has a long body and short legs. Her fur is brown. We call her Bear because she looks like a little bear. When Judy sits down, Bear sits by her.

To identify the main idea of the text, I will look at it again. The first sentence is about Judy having a new puppy. The other sentences tell more about the puppy, so the main idea is *Judy's new puppy.* Using information from the text, complete the Main Idea graphic organizer with children.

If... children have trouble understanding why Judy's new puppy is the main idea,
then... reread the first three sentences and ask, What are the sentences all about? *(Judy's new puppy)* This is the main idea.

On Their Own As children read "Favorite Colors" on Worktext p. 20 independently or with you, have them complete a Main Idea graphic organizer from p. 96. For additional practice, assign p. 21.

Mini-Lesson 2

Remind children that...
- the main idea is what the text is mostly about.
- details tell more about the main idea.

Guide Practice
Reread "My First Plane Ride" from p. T•16 aloud. What is the main idea? *(a first plane ride)* How do you know this is the main idea? *(Most of the sentences tell about the person taking a plane ride.)*

To find details, I look for sentences that give information about the main idea. One detail is that the person is visiting a grandmother. What are some other details? *(Possible answer: The person is taking a bag.)*

If... children have trouble identifying supporting details, **then...** focus on identifying the main idea. Then have children find sentences that tell more about the main idea.

On Their Own As children read "Eggs and Milk" on Worktext p. 22 independently or with you, have them complete a Main Idea and Supporting Details graphic organizer from p. 97. For additional practice, assign p. 23.

Mini-Lesson 3

Remind children that...
- the main idea is the most important idea in a text.
- supporting details describe or explain the main idea.

Guide Practice
Read the paragraph aloud.

Collecting Stamps

Many people like stamps. But how can you collect stamps without spending a lot of money? One way is to ask your friends and family to give you stamps they do not want. Another way is to trade with other people. Asking people to save stamps for you and trading stamps are easy ways to collect stamps. Before you know it, you will have more stamps than you can count!

Fill in a Main Idea and Details Organizer with children. What are most of the sentences in "Collecting Stamps" about? *(how to collect stamps without spending a lot of*

money) That is the main idea. What is one supporting detail? *(Ask people to give you stamps they don't want.)* Finish the organizer with children.

If... children have trouble identifying supporting details, **then...** encourage them to look for pieces of information that tell more about the main idea.

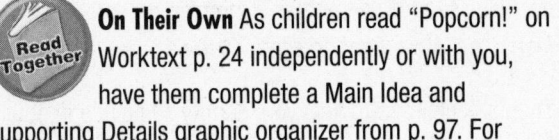

On Their Own As children read "Popcorn!" on Worktext p. 24 independently or with you, have them complete a Main Idea and Supporting Details graphic organizer from p. 97. For additional practice, assign p. 25.

Comprehension Lesson 5
Sequence

Objectives:
- Identify sequence of events.
- Identify sequence clue words.
- Organize events in sequence order.

MATERIALS

Worktext pp. 26–31
Story Sequence B Organizer, p. 99
Leveled Reader Database

Set the scene Explain to children that when they tell the sequence, or order of events, in a story, they tell what happens first, next, and last. Stories may have clue words, such as *first, next, then,* and *last.* To figure out the sequence of events in a story, picture the story in your mind.

Model Read aloud "Lily's New Brother." Ask children to listen closely to identify the sequence of events in the story.

Lily's New Brother

Two days ago I held my new baby brother for the first time. First, my mother told me to sit down. Then she put the baby in my arms. He was so small. Next, he grabbed my finger. He was small, but he was strong! Finally, he closed his eyes and fell asleep. My mother said I was going to be a great big sister.

Fill out the Story Sequence B Organizer with children. First, I write the title of the story in the *Title* box. To understand the story, I look for clue words that show the order in which things happen. I'm going to read the story again and picture what happens in my mind. What happens first? **Read the first sentence.** *(Lily's mother tells her to sit down.)* I write that in the *First* box.

I will think about the next thing that happens. I remember Lily's mother puts the baby in Lily's arms. I write that in the *Next* box. **Continue modeling how to add more events to the organizer in order.**

Mini-Lesson 1

Remind children that...
- in a story, something happens first, next, and last.
- sequence is the order in which things happen.

Guide Practice
Help children understand sequence by giving them everyday examples, such as a morning routine: *First, I wake up. Next, I get dressed. Then I eat breakfast.*

Then ask children to help you identify sequence in other sentences. Remind them to listen for clue words that show sequence.
First, Anna walked to the post office. Next, she mailed a package to her cousin. Then she walked home. What happens first? *(Anna went to the post office.)* What happens next? *(Anna mailed a package.)* What happens last? *(Anna walked home.)* As a group, work together to record the sequence.

Repeat the procedure with these sentences.
- *First, Chris bought some seeds at the store. Next, he planted the seeds in his backyard. Then he watered the seeds.*
- *The sky became dark. Then lightening lit up the sky. Next, raindrops started to fall.*

If... children have trouble identifying the sequence of events,

then... act out a basic process with a clear sequence, such as sharpening a pencil (put pencil in sharpener, turn handle, take pencil out).

Read Together **On Their Own** As children read "Ron and Charlie" on Worktext p. 26 independently or with you, have them complete a Story Sequence B graphic organizer on p. 99 to help them identify the sequence of events. For additional practice, assign p. 27.

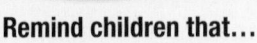

Mini-Lesson 2

Remind children that...
• sequence is the order of events.
• words such as *first, next, then,* and *last* show sequence.

Guide Practice

Explain that, when you tell what happens in a story, you tell the events in the correct sequence, or order.

Then write the following paragraph on the board and read it aloud. Remind children that clue words, such as *first, next,* and *then,* can help them identify sequence.

First, Sam and Matt walked to the lake. Next, they ate lunch by a tree. Then they changed into their swimming suits. Last, they jumped into the cool water.

What sequence clue words are in the paragraph? *(first, then, next, last)* Circle them. What happens first? *(Sam and Matt walked to the lake.)* How do you know? *(the clue word* first*)* Work with children to complete a

Story Sequence B graphic organizer using information from the text.

If... children have trouble identifying the second event, **then...** explain that not all events in a sequence will have clue words, but children can picture the events in their mind.

On Their Own As children read "The Cake Mystery" on Worktext p. 28 independently or with you, have them complete a Story Sequence B graphic organizer on from p. 99. For additional practice, assign p. 29.

Mini-Lesson 3

Remind children that...
• sequence is the order of events.
• clue words help identify sequence.
• they can organize events into sequence order.

Guide Practice

Tell children that good readers pay attention to when each event happens, or the sequence of events. Dates, times, and clue words, such as *first* and *last,* can help to identify sequence. Identify sequence to understand and remember text. When identifying sequence, tell only the most important events of the story.

Read aloud "The Special Olympics."

The Special Olympics

Eunice Kennedy Shriver had a sister with special needs. In 1962, Eunice started a day camp for children with special needs. It was called Camp Shriver.

In 1963, Shriver helped open 11 more camps around the country. In 1968, the first Special Olympic Games were held. Today many people from around the world have joined the Special Olympics.

What helps you identify sequence in the paragraph? *(dates)* To keep track of a sequence with dates, use an organizer. What happens first? *(1962: Eunice Shriver starts Camp Shriver.)* What happens next? *(1963: Mrs. Shriver opens 11 more camps.)* Complete a Story Sequence B Organizer with children.

If... children have trouble keeping track of sequence, **then...** help them identify the first and last event before identifying the events in between.

On Their Own As children read "George Washington" on Worktext p. 30 independently or with you, have them complete a Story Sequence B graphic organizer on p. 99. For additional practice, assign p. 31.

Objectives:
- Recognize traits of realistic stories.
- Recognize traits of fantasy.
- Distinguish between realism and fantasy.

MATERIALS

Worktext pp. 32–37
T-Chart, p. 100
Leveled Reader Database

Set the scene All stories are made-up. However, some stories tell about things that could happen in real life, and other stories tell about things that could not happen in real life. For example, I could come to school on a school bus, but I could not come to school in a time machine. As you read stories, decide if they could or could not really happen.

Model Read each story aloud.

Grandmother's Garden

May worked in the garden next to her grandmother. Grandmother was dirty from head to toe. Grandmother was busy planting flowers. She did not notice. "Grandmother, how did you get so dirty?" May asked.

Baby Bear's Soup

Mother Bear made a pot of soup. She added sticks and leaves to the pot. Then she gave some to Baby Bear. Baby Bear ate all the soup.

Use a T-Chart to list details to showcase the differences between realism and fantasy. I label the columns *Could Happen* and *Could Not Happen*. First, I look at "Grandmother's Garden." The first sentence says May worked next to Grandmother in the garden. That could happen, so I write it in the *Could Happen* column. Next, I look at the first sentence of "Baby Bear's Soup." It says Mother Bear is making soup. Why couldn't that happen? *(Bears don't cook.)* I write that in the *Could Not Happen* column. **Continue modeling.**

Mini-Lesson 1

Remind children that...
- all stories are made-up.
- some stories could really happen.
- some stories could not happen in real life.

Guide Practice

All stories are made up. You can look at details in a story to see if it could really happen or not.

Ask children whether the events in these sentences could really happen. Have them explain their answers.
- *Lara hid from the green dragon.* Could this happen in real life? *(no)* How do you know? *(Dragons are make-believe animals.)*
- *Cleo saw flames bursting through the windows of the building and smoke rising toward the sky.* Could this happen in real life? *(yes)* How do you know? *(A fire could happen.)*

- *Julio spread his arms and flew over the city.* Could this happen in real life? *(no)* How do you know? *(People cannot fly.)*

If... children have trouble distinguishing between realism and fantasy,

then... have them ask themselves if the details are things they might see in their own life or in others' lives, or if they would only happen in their imagination.

On Their Own As children read "Out of Sight" on Worktext p. 32 independently or with you, have them use the T-Chart on p. 100. For additional practice, assign p. 33.

Mini-Lesson 2

Remind children that…
- all stories are made-up.
- some stories could really happen, but others could not.

Guide Practice
Read the stories aloud and have children decide if each could really happen or not.

Missing: Bike

"Oh, no!" Nick had not put his bike in the garage. Nick looked in the yard. His bike was gone! Then Nick saw his bike in the house. His dad had put it away for him.

Missing: Flying Car

"Oh, no!" Amy had not put her flying car away. Amy looked for it. The flying car was gone! Then Amy's dad flew by in her own flying car. He said he had taken Amy's flying car to the shop.

Tell students to use a T-Chart to record details. In the first story, Nick is worried because he forgot to put away his bike. That could happen, so I write it in the *Could Happen* column.

In the second story, Amy is worried because she forgot to lock up her flying car. Flying cars are not real, so I write that in the *Could Not Happen* column. Continue modeling the stories using the T-Chart.

If… children have trouble distinguishing fantasy from realism,

then… reread the stories, explaining why each detail could or could not happen.

On Their Own As children read "Alive!" on Worktext p. 34 independently or with you, have them use the T-Chart on p. 100. For additional practice, assign p. 35.

Mini-Lesson 3

Remind children that…
- all stories are made-up.
- realistic stories could really happen.
- fantasies could not really happen.

Guide Practice
Help children understand that realistic stories are made-up, but they could happen in real life. Fantasies are made-up stories that include details that could not happen in real life. Fantasies can include both realistic and unrealistic details.

Read aloud the following story.

Seema bought a tree at the market. The gardener told her to water it often. Seema brought the tree home and forgot about it. The next week, Seema heard a knock at her door. She opened it, and the tree looked up at Seema. "You forgot about me! I am drying up out here!" Then the tree walked inside and got a glass of water from the kitchen.

Which details are realistic? *(Seema buying a tree at the market and forgetting about it)* Which details are fantastic? *(the tree talking, the tree getting a glass of water)* Is this a realistic story or a fantasy? *(fantasy)*

If… children have trouble identifying the story as fantasy,
then… remind them that a story with make-believe details is a fantasy.

On Their Own As children read "The Race" on Worktext p. 36 independently or with you, have them use the T-Chart on p. 100. For additional practice, assign p. 37.

Comprehension Lesson 7
Draw Conclusions

Objectives:

- Draw conclusions, or figure out more about, characters and events in a story or article.
- Use what you already know to help draw conclusions.
- Use evidence from the text to help draw conclusions.

MATERIALS

Worktext pp. 38–43
Three-Column Chart, p. 101
Leveled Reader Database

Set the scene Explain that, as children read a story or an article, they draw conclusions about what they read. Tell children that when they draw a conclusion, they figure something out about the characters and events. Readers draw conclusions by putting together what they read with what they know about real life.

Model Read aloud "Ana's Birthday Surprise."

Ana's Birthday Surprise

Ana invited all of her friends to her birthday party. On the day before the party, Ana decorated the yard. She planned games and made prizes. The next morning, Ana looked outside. It was raining. Tears ran down Ana's face. Then Ana heard people talking. She went downstairs to look. Ana's mother and sister were decorating inside. They had brought everything in before it rained. Ana smiled. The party would happen after all!

Display a Three-Column Chart from p. 101 with the headings *What I Know, What I Read,* and *My Conclusions.* I use a chart to draw conclusions. What conclusion can you draw about how Ana feels when she sees the rain?

First, I ask myself how people feel when they plan something outside and it rains. They usually feel sad. **Write this in the *What I Know* column.** Next, I check the story for details about how Ana feels. Ana spent a lot of time planning her party. When she sees the rain, tears run down her face. **Write this in the *What I Read* column.** To draw a conclusion, I put together what I know with what I read. I know people usually feel sad when rain ruins their plans. Ana cries when she sees the rain, so I draw the conclusion that Ana feels sad. **Write this in the *My Conclusions* column.**

Remind children that...

- drawing conclusions about a text means putting together what you know and what you read to figure something out.
- they draw conclusions in real life all the time.

Guide Practice

Imagine that your friend goes to the beach all day and comes back with a red face. You can put together what you already know about what happens when people stay in the sun too long with what you see to draw the conclusion that your friend got sunburned.

Ask children to put together what they know with what they hear in the sentences below to figure out what happened.

- *My dad was baking cookies. He grabbed the pan with his bare hand. Then he screamed.* What happened? *(The dad burned his hand on the hot pan.)*

- *Tony rides his bike to school, but he walked today. He said he couldn't play after school because he had to go to the bike repair shop.* What happened? *(Tony's bike is broken.)*

If... children have trouble understanding the concept of drawing conclusions,

then... offer additional real-life examples and remind children that in this context, *draw* means "to figure out," not "to create a picture."

On Their Own As children read "The Nest" on Worktext p. 38 independently or with you, have them complete a Three-Column Chart from p. 101 to help them draw conclusions. For additional practice, assign p. 39.

Mini-Lesson 2

Remind children that...
- drawing conclusions about a text means putting together what you know and what you read to figure something out.
- they can reread the text and check that their conclusions make sense.

Guide Practice
Reread "Ana's Birthday Surprise." Remind children about the conclusion that the rain made Ana sad. Note that sometimes people cry when they are happy. How do you know Ana is crying because she is sad and not because she is happy? Note that Ana spent the day before decorating for the outdoor party. It would be hard to have an outdoor party in the rain. So, it wouldn't make sense for Ana to be happy.

How do you think Ana feels when she sees her family decorating inside? Use the Three-Column Chart. I ask myself how people feel when others help them. They usually feel happy. Write this under *What I Know.* Then I check the story for details. Ana smiles. Write this under *What I Read.* I put that information together to draw the conclusion that Ana is happy. Write this under *My Conclusions.*

If... children have trouble drawing correct conclusions, **then...** display the story and circle details that help children answer the question.

 **On Their Own** As children read "The Laundry Basket" on Worktext p. 40 independently or with you, have them complete the Three-Column Chart. For additional practice, assign p. 41.

Mini-Lesson 3

Remind children that...
- drawing conclusions means putting together what you know and what you read or see to figure something out.
- they can draw conclusions about pictures, stories, and other texts, such as articles.

Guide Practice
Point out that children can—and already do—draw conclusions about everything from situations and pictures to stories and articles.

Read the paragraph aloud.

Hummingbirds

Hummingbirds are very small birds. Hummingbirds are small, but they eat a lot! Hummingbirds get most food from flowers. Sometimes they also eat bugs. Hummingbirds catch bugs by "hawking." Hawking happens when the hummingbird quickly flies down and catches a bug in its beak.

Ask: What conclusion can you draw about how *hawks* catch food? First, I ask myself what I already know about hawks. I know hawks are birds. Then I check the passage for details. The passage says *hawking* means quickly diving down to catch food. I put the information together to figure out that hawks must catch food by diving and grabbing it with their beak.

If... children have trouble understanding how you drew the conclusion above, **then...** model the process again, this time writing each piece of information in the appropriate column in a Three-Column Chart.

 **On Their Own** As children read "Giant Redwoods" on Worktext p. 42 independently or with you, have them complete the Three-Column Chart. For additional practice, assign p. 43.

Comprehension Lesson 8
Character

Objectives:
- Identify characters.
- Identify character traits.
- Recognize character motivation.

MATERIALS

Worktext pp. 44–49
Characters in a Story
Organizer, p. 93
Leveled Reader Database

Set the scene Explain to children that people and animals in a story are called characters. Authors usually name and describe the important characters in their stories. When you read a story, get to know each character by focusing on what each one says, does, and feels.

Model Read aloud "A New School."

A New School

It was Lori's first day in a new school. She was afraid. She walked into the classroom. She did not know what to do. The teacher smiled. She told Lori to sit at an empty desk.

Lori sat down. She looked to her right. There was a girl with red hair and glasses. She said her name was Jean. Jean had a lot of books on her desk. Jean asked, "Do you want to read together?"

Lori said, "Yes." Then she looked to her left. A boy with brown hair had a soccer shirt on. "I am Jack," he said. "Do you play soccer?"

Jean seemed nice, and Lori played soccer in her old school. Now Lori did not feel so afraid.

Tell children they can use a chart to identify and understand the characters. Display the Characters in a Story graphic organizer on p. 93. I'll reread the story again and listen for the first name I hear. Read the first two sentences of the first paragraph. First, I ask myself, *Who is mentioned?* Then, *What can I remember about that character?* The first sentence says Lori is a new student. I write this in my chart. Continue modeling, adding characters and details to the chart.

Mini-Lesson 1

Remind children that...
- people and animals in a story are characters.
- as they read, they can identify what characters say, do, and feel.

Guide Practice

Ask children to help you find other characters in the story "A New School." Reread the first paragraph. Who is mentioned? What can you remember about each character? As a group, work together to write the next character and something to remember about him or her. *(Possible answer: Character: the teacher; What I remember: smile)*

Repeat the procedure above for the next two paragraphs. Possible responses:
- Character: Jean; What I remember: girl, red hair, glasses, likes to read

- Character: Jack; What I remember: boy, likes soccer, brown hair

If... children have trouble identifying the characters in a story,
then... reread a sentence and ask: *Is a person mentioned in the sentence? What can you remember about this character?*

On Their Own As children read "The Jones Family" on Worktext p. 44 independently or with you, have them complete a Characters in a Story graphic organizer on p. 93 to help them identify characters. For additional practice, assign p. 45.

Mini-Lesson 2

Remind children that...

- they can identify the people and animals, or characters, in a story.
- they can describe how each character looks and acts.

Guide Practice

Read aloud "At the Market."

At the Market

My family sells vegetables at the market. When we get there, Mother talks to the other people. She talks and laughs a lot.

Father puts out the vegetables. He cleans each one. He places them in rows. People tell him his vegetables are the best. Then he smiles.

My little brother runs around the market until dark. He stops to pet any dog he sees. At last, my parents call him to go home.

Explain that you will figure out who the characters are and describe them. Reread the first paragraph. I first ask, *Who is the first character?* Then, *What does she do? What is she like?* The first paragraph says that Mother talks and laughs. I write this in the Characters in a Story organizer. Repeat the procedure for the other characters.

If... children have trouble describing characters, **then...** ask *What is this person like? What does he or she do?*

On Their Own As children read "Maria's Visit" on Worktext p. 46 independently or with you, have them complete a Characters in a Story organizer on p. 93. For additional practice, assign p. 47.

Mini-Lesson 3

Remind children that...

- they can describe characters by identifying how they look and act.
- they can identify the reasons characters act the way they do.

Guide Practice

Explain that a character's traits describe how the character looks and acts. Character motivation is a character's reasons for acting a certain way. For example, in "A New School," Jean's traits are her curly red hair and glasses. Her motivation for talking to Lori might be to make friends or to find a study partner.

Read the following text aloud.

Oscar's hair fell over his eyes. He was the shortest boy in class. Yet, he tried out for the basketball team. People laughed because they thought he was too short. Oscar

just smiled. When he had the ball, no one could get it from him. He passed the ball quickly to his teammates. Oscar made the team.

Ask, What are Oscar's traits? *(messy hair, short, good at basketball)* What is his motivation for trying out for basketball? *(to make the team, to prove others wrong)*

If... children have trouble identifying character motivation,
then... as a group list the reasons why a character acts a certain way.

On Their Own As children read "Under the Bed" on Worktext p. 48 independently or with you, have them complete a Characters in a Story organizer on p. 93. For additional practice, assign p. 49.

Comprehension Lesson 9
Plot

Objectives:
- Identify the plot, or what happens, in a story.
- Recognize the beginning, middle, and ending of a story.
- Identify the problem and solution in a story.

MATERIALS
Worktext pp. 50–55
Events in a Story Organizer, p. 94
Leveled Reader Database

Set the scene Explain that the plot is what happens in a story, or the important events. The plot in each story has a beginning, middle, and end. Most events in a story are related to a problem. Other events are related to a solution to the problem. Children should identify the events of the plot to better understand what they read.

Model Read aloud "Honey."

Honey

Last summer Jack stayed at his grandfather's farm. On the first day, he did not do much. On the second day, Jack walked into the barn. He saw a tiny kitten. It was crying. It looked hungry.

Jack's grandfather showed him how to feed the kitten. He said Jack could keep the kitten if he took care of it.

Every day Jack gave the kitten food. Jack also cleaned the cat's fur. He named the kitten Honey.

Jack's parents let him keep Honey. Now Honey follows Jack around the house.

Explain that children can use an Events in a Story organizer on p. 94 to help them understand this story. I write the title, "Honey," in the *Title* box. Then I think about the first thing that happens. I remember Jack goes to his grandfather's farm. I write that in the *First Event* box.

Then I think about the next important thing that happens. I remember that Jack finds a crying kitten in the barn. I write that in the *Next Event* box. Continue modeling, writing in each important event.

Remind children that...
- an event is something that happens in a story.
- they can keep track of the order of events to better understand a story.

Guide Practice
Help children understand that they do not need to identify every event in the plot. They should only focus on the most important events. For example, Jack finding the kitten is an event, but the kitten looking hungry is not an event.

Ask children to help you find other important events in the story "Honey" and record them in the organizer. Reread paragraphs as necessary. What's the next thing that happens? Then what happens? As a group, work together to write the next event. (Possible response: Jack's grandfather shows him how to feed the kitten.) Repeat the procedure for the next and last event.

Possible responses:
- *Next Event:* Jack takes care of the kitten.
- *Last Event:* Jack takes Honey home with him.

If... children have trouble identifying plot,
then... review the events in the story and have children tell the events in their own words.

On Their Own As children read "Tomatoes" on Worktext p. 50 independently or with you, have them complete an Events in a Story organizer on p. 94 to help them keep track of important events. For additional practice, assign p. 51.

Mini-Lesson 2

Remind children that...
- a plot is the important events that happen in a story.
- a plot has a beginning, middle, and end.

Guide Practice

Explain that good readers identify and describe the plot to better understand a story.

Read the story aloud. Have children listen for the plot.

A Great Summer

School was almost over. Amita and Jane talked about day camp, swimming, and jumping rope. "This will be a great summer!" they said.

The very next day Amita fell and broke her arm. She had to wear a cast. "Oh no! This will be a bad summer," said Amita.

Jane went to see Amita every day. They played games and read fun books. It was a great summer after all.

Show an Events in a Story organizer on p. 94. To describe the plot, I write what happens in the beginning, the middle, and the end. In the beginning, Amita and Jane talk about their summer plans. Write this in the organizer. Next, I think about the middle of the story. Continue modeling until the organizer is completed.

If... children have trouble keeping track of important events,

then... encourage them to write down the events in order in an organizer or list.

 **On Their Own** As children read "Something New" on Worktext p. 52 independently or with you, have them complete an Events in a Story organizer on p. 94. For additional practice, assign p. 53.

Mini-Lesson 3

Remind children that...
- events in the beginning, middle, and end of a story make up the plot.
- a plot includes a problem and a solution.

Guide Practice

Explain that most stories are about a problem. Most of the events in a story are related to that problem. Other events are related to the problem's solution.

Read the story aloud. Have children listen for the plot's problem and solution.

The Flower Garden

Carlos planted a flower garden. He watered his flowers, and they grew.

Then the flowers stopped growing. Carlos watched the garden day and night. At night he saw rabbits eating his flowers.

Carlos wanted his flowers to grow, but he didn't want to hurt the rabbits. Carlos built a fence and put it around his flowers. Then the flowers grew again.

First, display an Events in a Story organizer on p. 94. Model how to describe what happens in the beginning, middle, and end of the story. What is the problem in the story? *(Rabbits eat the flowers.)* What is the solution? *(Carlos builds a fence.)*

If... children have trouble identifying the problem and solution,

then... have them focus on describing the events in order first and then decide which event is the problem and which is the solution.

 **On Their Own** As children read "Lost and Found" on Worktext p. 54 independently or with you, have them complete an Events in a Story organizer. For additional practice, assign p. 55.

Comprehension Lesson 10
Setting

Objectives:
- Identify where and when a story takes place.
- Distinguish between real and imaginary settings.
- Determine how setting relates to other story elements, such as character and plot.

MATERIALS

Worktext pp. 56–61
Setting of a Story Organizer, p. 98
Leveled Reader Database

Set the scene Explain that the setting is when and where a story takes place. Settings can be real or make-believe. In some stories, setting is important to the characters or plot. As children read, they should look for details that tell about the setting.

Model Read aloud "Summer Camp."

Summer Camp

Last summer Charlie went to summer camp. It is a camp for children who like to sing and dance.

The camp is in the mountains by a lake. It has big cabins made of wood. Huge trees surround the camp. Charlie and his friends liked to run in the large field.

Use the Setting of a Story Organizer on p. 98 to help figure out the setting with children. I can reread the story and listen for details about time and place. **Read the first paragraph.** First, I ask, "Where is the story happening?" In the first sentence, it says Charlie went to summer camp. Then I ask, "When is the story happening?" The first sentence says Charlie went last summer. I write this in the *Time* and *Place* boxes in the chart.

Read the second paragraph. I look for details about the setting. The second paragraph says the camp is in the mountains. I write that information in the *Detail* box. **Continue modeling.**

Mini-Lesson 1

Remind children that...
- they can identify where and when a story takes place.
- a story can happen in a real or make-believe time and place.

Guide Practice

Help children understand how to identify where and when a story takes place by giving examples.
- *Last Sunday, Johnny walked his dog down Main Street. It was raining, so the street was quiet.* Where does the story happen? *(on Main Street)* When does it happen? *(last Sunday)*
- *Carmen met some friendly unicorns in a magic forest 100 years ago. She showed them her talking frog.* Where does the story happen? *(a magic forest)* When does it happen? *(100 years ago)*

Which of the stories could be about a real time and place? *(the first story)*

Which of the stories is about a make-believe place? *(the second one)* How do you know? *(It is happening in a magic forest and includes unicorns and a talking frog.)*

If... children have trouble identifying where and when stories take place,
then... have them reread, circling clues that give details about place and time.

On Their Own As children read "The Ocean" on Worktext p. 56 independently or with you, have them complete a Setting of a Story Organizer from p. 98. For additional practice, assign p. 57.

Mini-Lesson 2

Remind children that...
- the setting is where and when a story takes place.
- a setting can be real or make-believe.
- they can picture the setting in their minds to better remember it.

Guide Practice

Tell children that the setting is where and when a story happens. To identify setting, find details about where and when the story happens. Tell children that good readers picture the setting in their minds as they read.

Then read aloud the story.

At the Barn

Every morning Karen feeds chickens. They walk all over the big red barn. Then they run to Karen for breakfast. In the high roof of the barn, there are other birds. They sing and move their wings.

Model how to fill out the Setting of a Story Organizer from p. 98. First, I ask "What time and place are talked about?" The time is every morning. The place is a barn. I write that in the *Time* and *Place* boxes. Next, I ask, "What is inside the barn?" There are chickens and birds. I write that in a *Detail* box. Continue modeling.

If... children have trouble describing the setting, **then...** ask such questions as "What does the writer say about the barn?" and "What does it look like?"

 **On Their Own** Have children read "Laura's Room" on Worktext p. 58 independently or with you, filling out the Setting of a Story Organizer as they read. For additional practice, assign p. 59.

Mini-Lesson 3

Remind children that...
- the setting is where and when a story takes place.
- a setting can be real or make-believe.

Guide Practice

Help children understand that setting can affect other parts of a story, such as character or plot. In some stories, a different setting changes the story completely.

Read aloud "The Jungle."

The Jungle

A monkey lives in the jungle. There are many tall trees and flowers. There is a lot of different fruit to eat. When it rains, the monkey hides under the trees. He always has enough food.

Model how to fill out the Setting of a Story graphic organizer on p. 98. Then ask: How is the setting in "The Jungle" related to the character? *(The jungle is the monkey's home and gives him food.)* How would the story be different if the setting were a big city? *(Possible response: The monkey might not have a home or get enough food.)*

If... children have trouble understanding how a new setting would change the story,
then... encourage them to picture in their minds the story in the new setting.

On Their Own Have children read "Aunt Ida's" on Worktext p. 60 independently or with you, using the Setting of a Story organizer. For additional practice, assign p. 61.

Comprehension Lesson 11
Retell/Summarize

Objectives:
- Retell key events in a story in order.
- Summarize the main ideas of a nonfiction text.

Set the scene Explain to children that when you summarize nonfiction or retell a story, you briefly tell what happens—or what it is mostly about—in your own words.

Model To model retelling fiction, first read aloud "The Ugly Duckling."

The Ugly Duckling

Mother Duck had seven eggs. Six were small, and one was very big. One morning, six yellow baby ducks popped out from the small eggs. Then a big gray baby duck came out of the last egg. He was not pretty. The other ducks laughed at him. He felt sad.

He left the farm to find another duck that looked like him. He could not find any. Then he saw some beautiful white swans in the sky. "If only I could look like them!" he said.

A few weeks later the duck saw himself in a pond. "Oh! I look so different!" He looked up. There was a group of beautiful swans. Then the duck knew he was a beautiful swan too.

Tell students that to retell a story, you only focus on the important events. Model how to use the Events in a Story Organizer on p. 94 to retell. First, I write the title. Then I think about the first key event that happens. I remember that Mother Duck has seven eggs, and one egg is different. I write that in the *First Event* box.

What happens next? A big gray baby duck hatches, but he's not pretty like the others. I write that in the *Next Event* box. Continue modeling how to choose key events and write them in order in the organizer.

MATERIALS

Worktext pp. 62–67
Events in a Story Organizer, p. 94
Story Sequence B Organizer, p. 99
Routine Cards 15 and 16
Leveled Reader Database

Mini-Lesson 1

Remind children that...
- retelling a story means telling the events of the story in order.
- retelling helps readers remember what they read.
- they should use their own words to retell a story.

Guide Practice

Help children understand identifying key events and retelling them in order. Retell what you did this morning before getting to school. Tell children that words such as *first, next,* and *last* are clue words about the order of events. For example, say: *This morning I took a shower and got dressed. Next, I ate breakfast. Last, I drove to school.*

Ask children to help you tell what happened in order, using an Events in a Story Organizer from p. 94. What was the first thing that happened? *(The teacher took a shower and got dressed.)* I write that in the organizer

under *First Event.* What happened after that? *(The teacher ate breakfast.)* I write that in the organizer. What was the last event that happened? *(The teacher drove to school.)*

If... children have trouble retelling events in order, **then...** have them focus on finding clue words first.

On Their Own As children read "Hot or Not?" on Worktext p. 62 independently or with you, have them complete an Events in a Story Organizer to practice retelling. For additional practice, assign p. 63.

Mini-Lesson 2

Remind children that...

- retelling a story means telling story events in the correct order.
- summarizing nonfiction means telling the important ideas in your own words.

Guide Practice

Tell children that when they summarize nonfiction, they should focus only on important ideas. Ask yourself, "What is the passage mostly about?" If children need to review main ideas and details, revisit Lesson 4. Read aloud "Dwarf Hamsters."

Dwarf Hamsters

Dwarf hamsters are only about 3 inches long. They come in many colors. They have short heads and very small ears. A dwarf hamster can live by itself or share a cage with another dwarf hamster. If the hamsters get upset, they make noise. Dwarf hamsters rarely fight. They make good pets.

First, I try to figure out what this passage is about in one or two words. I see that it's about dwarf hamsters. Then I try to find the most important idea about dwarf hamsters. The author gives many facts, but the most important idea is that the hamsters make good pets. What are some reasons dwarf hamsters make good pets? (They are small, they look interesting, and they rarely fight.)

To summarize, I will say the most important idea and the reasons. Dwarf hamsters make good pets because they are small, look interesting, and rarely fight.

If... children have trouble summarizing the passage, **then...** reread the passage and use Routine Card 16.

 **On Their Own** Have children practice retelling fiction by reading "Dinner Time" on Worktext p. 64 independently or with you. Have them fill out the Story Sequence B Organizer. For summarizing nonfiction, assign p. 65.

Mini-Lesson 3

Remind children that...

- retelling a story means telling story events in the correct order.
- summarizing nonfiction means telling the important ideas in your own words.
- summaries should not be more than a few sentences.

Guide Practice

Tell children that they will practice summarizing nonfiction. Explain that the first step in summarizing is identifying what the passage is mostly about. If children need to review main ideas and details, revisit Lesson 4. Read aloud "Volunteer Day."

Volunteer Day

Many schools have a Volunteer Day. On this special day, children work to improve their neighborhoods or help their neighbors. For example, some children clean up parks or turn old lots into beautiful gardens. Other

children help take care of animals at an animal shelter. Sometimes, children visit senior citizens and perform a play for them or read books together.

- What is the passage mostly about? *(how children help their communities on Volunteer Day)*
- What are some examples of what children do on Volunteer Day? (clean up parks, build gardens, help out at animal shelters, spend time with senior citizens)

To summarize, I will say the most important idea and the reasons. On Volunteer Days, children help make their neighborhoods a better place. They clean up parks, help at animal shelters, or spend time with senior citizens.

If... children have trouble identifying the main idea, **then...** use Routine Card 16.

 **On Their Own** Have children retell fiction by reading "Cinderella" on Worktext p. 66 independently or with you. For practice summarizing nonfiction, assign p. 67.

Background Knowledge

Objectives:
- Recognize and use background knowledge to connect to a new story or article.
- Use background knowledge to monitor understanding while reading.

MATERIALS

Worktext pp. 68–73
T-Chart, p. 100
Leveled Reader Database

Set the scene Explain to children that, as they read, they often use background knowledge to connect to and better understand what they read. Background knowledge is what they already know about a topic through their own experiences or other readings. For example, they might have done something similar to what a character in a story does. They might have felt the same way that a character feels. Or, children might read about a topic, such as dogs, that they have already read about or seen in their own lives.

Model Read aloud the first paragraph of "A New Box of Crayons."

A New Box of Crayons

Carla loves new crayons. She got a new box for her birthday. She could not wait to use them! Carla has a twin sister, Sandra. Sandra also got new crayons. But Sandra did not use her crayons right away.

Carla sat down at the table. Then she got out her new crayons and paper. She drew a flower garden. She colored the grass and trees. She colored the flowers.

Help children fill in a T-Chart from p. 100. Write the labels *Story Events* and *My Experiences* on the top columns of the chart. I'm going to compare the events in this story with my own experiences. Like Carla, I love getting a new box of crayons. All of the crayons are sharp and ready to use. I write that on both sides of the chart. **Write on the left:** *Carla loves new crayons.* Write on the right: *I love new crayons.* Carla has a twin sister. I also have a sister. I write that in the chart.

Mini-Lesson 1

Remind children that...
- their background knowledge is what they already know about something.
- using background knowledge helps them understand what they read.

Guide Practice

Read aloud the next part of "A New Box of Crayons."

Carla took out her green crayon. The tip was broken! She opened Sandra's box. Carla saw the green one. It was not broken. She took it out. She started to color with it. Just then, Sandra walked in the room.

Sandra was angry because Carla used her crayon without asking. Carla told her what happened. Then she said she was sorry. Sandra said it was okay after all.

Help children apply background knowledge. What does Carla do? *(She takes something that isn't hers.)* Add this

to the chart. When have you taken something that didn't belong to you? Add children's answers to the chart. How did you feel in that situation? How do you think Carla feels? How do you think Sandra feels? Continue adding answers to the chart.

If... children have trouble connecting with the text, **then...** ask such questions as, "What does this remind you of in your own life?" and "How would you feel in this situation?"

On Their Own As children read "We Wait" on Worktext p. 68 independently or with you, have them complete a T-Chart from p. 100. For additional practice, assign p. 69.

Mini-Lesson 2

Remind children that...

- they can compare new stories to stories they have already read to better understand them.
- using background knowledge can help them know what to expect in new stories.

Guide Practice

Read aloud the familiar nursery rhyme.

Little Miss Muffet

Little Miss Muffet
Sat on a tuffet
Eating her curds and whey.
Along came a spider,
Who sat down beside her
And frightened Miss Muffet away.

Now read aloud "Along Came a Spider."

Along Came a Spider

The children were playing outside. They ran past a barn. They jumped on some leaves. Just then, they saw a black spider. It was moving toward them. The children screamed. Then they ran home.

Show children how knowing one story can help them understand a new story. How did "Along Came a Spider" remind you of "Little Miss Muffet"? Ask students how the characters, settings, and events of the stories are alike and different and fill in a T-Chart from p. 100.

If... children have trouble comparing a familiar story to a new one,

then... ask questions, such as "How is Miss Muffet like the children in 'Along Came a Spider'?" and "How are their actions similar?"

 **On Their Own** Have children read "Hickory Dickory Dock" on Worktext p. 70 independently or with you, filling out the T-Chart. For additional practice, assign p. 71.

Mini-Lesson 3

Remind children that...

- their background knowledge is what they already know or have read about a topic.
- using background knowledge can help them connect to and better understand stories or articles they read.

Guide Practice

Read the first paragraph of the article aloud.

A couple and their dog were camping last week. They went hiking in the woods. Then, on the path, they saw a mountain lion. Mountain lions are usually afraid of people, but they can be dangerous.

The lion started to come near the people, but their dog scared it away. The people were not hurt.

Ask students: What do you know about how dogs behave when their owners are in danger? *(They are protective.)* Based on what you know about dogs, how would you

expect this dog to act? *(The dog would probably protect its owners.)*

Read the second paragraph aloud. How did your background knowledge help you understand the article? *(Knowing how dogs usually act helps readers understand this dog's actions.)*

If... children have trouble understanding how to apply background knowledge,

then... have them ask, "What do I already know about this topic?" as they read.

On Their Own Have children read "Tulips and Daffodils" on Worktext p. 72 independently or with you, using the T-Chart. For additional practice, assign p. 73.

Comprehension Lesson 13
Questioning

Objectives:

- Ask *who, what, when, where, why,* and *how* questions about a text.
- Ask questions to help clarify the text.
- Reread parts of the text to help answer questions and to monitor comprehension.

MATERIALS

Worktext pp. 74–79
T-Chart, p. 100
Leveled Reader Database

Set the scene Tell children that good readers keep track of what they read to better remember and understand it. For example, when they read a story, they keep track of who the characters are, what they do, why they do what they do, and how things happen. They also keep track of where and when the story takes place. To answer their questions, they reread the text.

Model Read aloud "Will's Train Ride."

Will's Train Ride

Will went on his first train ride last week. He and his grandfather took the train into the city. When they boarded the train, they climbed the steps and sat in the top row. The train roared down the tracks. They passed many houses and stores. At last, the train pulled into the city. Will was excited. There were a lot of cars, trucks, and buses on the street. Will and his grandfather walked to a park. There they ate lunch. After their day, they took the train home. What a fun first ride!

Display a T-Chart for children from p. 100. Label the columns *Question* and *Answer.* To help me understand this story, I use a chart to record questions and answers. First, I ask, *When and where does the story take place?* The first sentence says last week. Most of the story takes place on a train to the city. Record the question and answer in the chart.

Who are the characters? The first two sentences talk about Will and his grandfather. *What do the characters do?* They take a train to the city. Continue modeling with children, recording questions and answers in the chart.

Mini-Lesson 1

Remind children that...

- asking and answering *who, what, when, where, why,* and *how* questions will help them understand what they read.
- they should reread parts of the text to answer their questions.

Guide Practice

Give children practice questioning.

- This morning Meg went to the store to buy cat food for her kitten Toby. When she got home, Toby was chasing a fly in the kitchen.
- What questions could you ask? *(Possible questions: Who is in the story? What happens?)* Record the questions in a chart. Then have children answer them. *(Meg and Toby are in the story. Meg buys cat food and sees Toby chasing a fly.)*
- Juan saw a boy fall off his bike when he hit a rock. Juan ran inside and called his dad for help.

- What *why* and *how* questions could you ask? *(Why did the boy fall off his bike? How does Juan help the boy?)* How would you answer them? *(The boy hit a rock. Juan called his dad.)*

If... children have trouble identifying which questions to ask,

then... remind them of the 5 Ws and H: *who, what, where, when, why,* and *how.*

Read Together **On Their Own** As children read "Ann's Birthday Party" on Worktext p. 74 independently or with you, have them complete a T-Chart from p. 100. For additional practice, assign p. 75.

Mini-Lesson 2

Remind children that...

- they can ask clarifying questions to better understand what they read.
- they can ask questions before, during, and after reading.

Guide Practice

Read "The Reef" aloud.

The Reef

The sea looks quiet. The sea looks still. What is going on under the water? Come find out! You can find a reef in warm water. Under the water, beautiful fish live on the reef. They come in all sizes and colors. Plants and other animals live there too.

Guide children to stop and ask questions before, during, and after they read to check comprehension. *To make sure I understand what I read, I ask questions about*

anything that was confusing. *For example, which words are new to me? (Possible answer: reef)* How can I find out the meaning of this word? *(Look in a dictionary.)* Then ask other clarifying questions, such as, *What is the paragraph mostly about?*

If... children have trouble remembering questions to ask after they read,

then... encourage them to write down questions as they read and then reread the text to try to answer them.

 **On Their Own** Have children read "What Happened?" on Worktext p. 76 independently or with you, filling out the T-Chart from p. 100 as they read. For additional practice, assign p. 77.

Mini-Lesson 3

Remind children that...

- they can ask clarifying questions to better understand the meaning of a story or article.
- they can answer their questions by rereading parts of the text.

Guide Practice

Read "Helping Out."

Helping Out

Katie's older brother Aaron was making a set for a school play. "Can I help?" she asked.

"You can help by making me a sun to hang from the ceiling," said Aaron. Katie was happy to help, but she was not sure how to make the sun.

Pause to remind children to ask themselves questions. For example, ask: How does Katie feel about making the

sun? *(She is glad to help, but she isn't sure how to do it.)* Finish reading.

Then she had an idea. Katie got a large bowl and traced a circle on some white paper. Then she colored the circle yellow and cut it out. Last, Katie glued string to the back so it could hang from the ceiling.

"Perfect!" Aaron said.

Ask children to come up with their own clarifying questions and answers about the text.

If... children have trouble answering their questions,
then... have them find the answers by rereading the text.

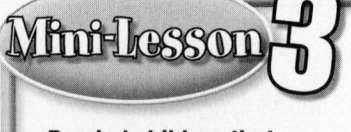 **On Their Own** Have children read "Carmen's Noisy Day" on Worktext p. 78 independently or with you, using a T-Chart from p. 100. For additional practice, assign p. 79.

Comprehension Lesson 14
Important Ideas

Objectives:

- Recognize important ideas in a text.
- Distinguish important ideas from minor details.
- Identify and support important ideas with facts and details from the text.

MATERIALS

Worktext pp. 80–85
T-Chart Organizer, p. 100
Web, p. 102
Leveled Reader Database

Set the scene Important ideas are the essential ideas and supporting details in a selection. Important ideas include information that gives clues to the author's purpose, or reason for writing. To find important ideas, look for the essential ideas in the text as well as at the titles, signal words, illustrations, photographs, and graphic sources.

Model Read aloud "Flying Squirrels."

Flying Squirrels

Flying squirrels look like they fly. But they do not fly at all! Instead, they sail from tree to tree. Flying squirrels look like other squirrels, but they are very thin. They also have a piece of thin fur between their front and back legs. This helps them become flat, like a piece of paper. First, the squirrel jumps into the air. Then, it spreads its legs and tail. It uses its tail to move right or left. Last, the squirrel lands on all four feet. Some flying squirrels land on the ground. They look for food there.

Display a Web. Label the center oval *Important Idea* and the outer ovals *Supporting Detail*. I can use a Web to record important ideas. I ask myself, "What are the essential ideas in this article?" I know the title is "Flying Squirrels" and those words are repeated in the article. What is the author saying about flying squirrels? The first two sentences say that flying squirrels look like they fly, but they actually just sail through the air. That must be an important idea. I can tell it is important because the rest of the article supports that idea by explaining how they sail through the air.

Remind children that...

- important ideas are the major ideas in a text.
- titles, bold words, and graphic sources give clues to important ideas.
- they can distinguish important ideas and details from minor details.

Guide Practice

Reread "Flying Squirrels" for students. What facts are in the text? *(Possible responses: Flying squirrels are very thin. They have a piece of fur between their front and back legs that helps them become flat. They use their tail to move left or right.)* Record these details in the outer ovals of the Web. What do these facts tell you about flying squirrels? *(They explain how flying squirrels are able to glide or sail in the air.)* Each fact supports the important idea that flying squirrels sail in the air.

What detail is *not* important? *(Some flying squirrels look for food on the ground.)* Why isn't this detail important? *(It doesn't help the reader understand the text.)*

If... children have trouble identifying important ideas, **then...** have them circle the title, any boldface or repeated words, and ask themselves, *What is the author saying about this?*

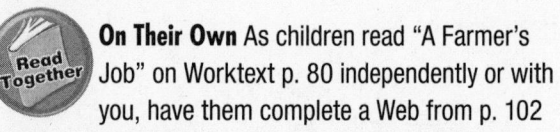

On Their Own As children read "A Farmer's Job" on Worktext p. 80 independently or with you, have them complete a Web from p. 102 to help them identify important ideas. For additional practice, assign p. 81.

Mini-Lesson 2

Remind children that...
- important ideas are the major ideas in a text.
- they can use facts and details to help identify and support important ideas.

Guide Practice
Read the article aloud.

The Driest Place on Earth

No place on Earth is as dry as the Atacama Desert. It is hundreds of miles long. Some parts have not had rain for many years. Few animals live there. Few plants grow there. The land is brown. Yet, this desert is not like most dry places. It is next to an ocean. Also, the desert is not hot. It stays cool in summer. The ocean keeps the air cool. There is little rain. But, there is a lot of fog. It comes from the ocean. People catch water from the fog. Then they save the water. They use it for drinking and cleaning. Many people live in this dry place.

Ask: What is important to know? *(The Atacama Desert is the driest place on Earth.)* What facts and details support this idea? *(The desert is near an ocean, it isn't hot, and it has fog.)*

If... children have trouble identifying important ideas, **then...** have them first identify facts and details.

 **On Their Own** Have children read "Hamsters Make Good Pets" on Worktext p. 82 independently or with you, using the T-Chart from p. 100. For additional practice, assign p. 83.

Mini-Lesson 3

Remind children that...
- important ideas are the major ideas in a text.
- important ideas are supported by facts and details in the rest of the text.

Guide Practice
Read "Homes of Animals" aloud.

Homes of Animals

Badgers live under the ground. Their homes usually have one opening that leads to a sleeping room. Some badger homes can be very large. They may have up to 100 openings and two levels.

Beavers can live in rivers, lakes, and ponds. Their homes are made out of sticks and mud. They are shaped like cones. Beaver homes can be as tall as 10 feet high and as wide as 20 feet.

Create a Web. What facts are in the first paragraph? *(Badgers live under the ground; their homes may have up to 100 openings and two levels.)* Record the responses in the Web and repeat the procedure for the second paragraph. What important idea do the facts support? *(Possible answer: Animals have different types of homes.)*

If... children have trouble identifying the important idea, **then...** remind them to look at text features such as titles and repeated words.

On Their Own Have children read "Cell Phones" on Worktext p. 84 independently or with you, filling out a Web from p. 102. For additional practice, assign p. 85.

Objectives:
- Visualize a story, or create a mental picture of it.
- Identify descriptive details that help readers visualize a story.

MATERIALS

Worktext pp. 86–91
Five-Box Chart, p. 95
Leveled Reader Database

Set the scene Explain that when readers visualize a story or article, they create a picture of it in their minds. When we picture a story in our minds, we use our senses. We try to see what is happening, smell the smells, hear the sounds, and so on. Visualizing helps us better remember and enjoy what we read.

Model Read the story aloud. Have children close their eyes to visualize as you read.

The Little Green Apple

Mike walked to the garden with his grandmother. The long grass was cool and wet on his legs. Grandmother opened the gate to the garden. A blue bird sang to them. It was on an old apple tree inside the gate. "Well, hello there," said Grandmother to the bird. The bird sang once more. Then it hid in its nest. Inside the garden, Mike saw rows and rows of tall green plants. Flowers grew in red and yellow. Grandmother picked an apple from the tree. She gave it to Mike. "Try this," she said. Mike took a bite. The little green apple tasted cold and sweet.

After reading, have children open their eyes. Display a Five-Box Chart from p. 95 with each sense listed as a chart head. What did you see in your mind as you heard the story? I saw a blue bird, a garden, red and yellow flowers, and a little green apple. I write these in the chart under *See*. Then I can draw pictures to help me remember. Continue modeling with the other senses.

Mini-Lesson 1

Remind children that...
- to visualize means to create a picture in your mind.
- when we visualize, we use our senses.

Guide Practice

Have children close their eyes and picture each passage as you read it aloud.

- *Jan's cake turned golden brown as it baked. She opened the oven door. Jan closed her eyes and smelled the warm, sweet scent that filled the kitchen.* What did you picture in your mind? *(the cake turning brown in the oven)* What do you know about cakes when they bake? *(Cakes turn brown and smell sweet.)* What senses helped you picture the text? *(sight, smell)*
- *Freddie felt his cat brush past his legs. She meowed loudly. Freddie poured her a bowl of smooth, creamy milk.* What did you picture in your mind? *(the cat*

brushing past Freddie's legs, the bowl of milk) What do you know about cats when they are hungry? *(They meow.)* What senses helped you visualize the text? *(sight, touch, sound)*

If... children have trouble identifying which senses are engaged,
then... discuss individual details, pointing out clue words, such as *smell* and *felt*.

On Their Own Have children read "Fishing Trip" on Worktext p. 86 independently or with you. For additional practice, assign p. 87 and have them complete the Five-Box Chart from p. 95.

Mini-Lesson 2

Remind children that...

- to visualize means to create a picture in the mind.
- as they read, they can refine and revise what they visualize to match the author's descriptions in the text.

Guide Practice

Read aloud the beginning of a story below.

Sam's mother had a surprise for him. Sam closed his eyes. They got in the car and drove. Then they got out. Sam heard people talking and a dog barking. He thought they were at a park.

Ask: What did you picture in your mind? *(Sam with his eyes closed in a car and then in a park.)* Finish the story.

"Open your eyes!" Sam was in his own yard! They had just driven around the block. "Happy Birthday!" his friends yelled. Then a big, furry dog ran to Sam. "There's your present!" said his mother.

As you read, revise the picture in your mind to match the text. How did your picture of the story change? *(The park changed to Sam's yard, and the sights and sounds became those of Sam's friends and new dog.)*

If... children have trouble visualizing how the story changed,

then... have them think about events that happened later in the story.

 **On Their Own** Have children read "Watering the Flowers" on Worktext p. 88 independently or with you. For additional practice, assign p. 89 and have children fill out the Five-Box Chart from p. 95.

Mini-Lesson 3

Remind children that...

- they can use all five senses to visualize text.
- identifying descriptive details helps readers visualize text.

Guide Practice

Read the text aloud to students.

Easy Apple Pie

Making apple pie is easy. First, roll half the dough until it is smooth. Then push it into the pie pan. Have a parent cut apples into pieces. Put them in the pan. Add flour, sugar, and spices. Then press more dough on top. Set your timer and have a parent cook the pie for 40 minutes or until the pie is light brown. When the timer rings, have a parent take out the pie. By now, the kitchen will smell like baked apples. When the pie is cool to the touch, have a parent cut it in pieces. Enjoy the sweet taste!

Display a Five-Box Chart from p. 95 and use each sense as a box heading. Have children identify the descriptive details that describe each sense and record them in the correct box.

If... children have trouble visualizing specific descriptive details,

then... record the text on the board, help children circle each detail, and have them identify the sense each describes.

On Their Own Have children read "The Garage Sale" on Worktext p. 90 independently or with you. For additional practice, assign p. 91 and have children use the Five-Box Chart.

Comprehension
Student Worktext

Name _____

Read the story.

> ## Before the Storm
> ### by Emma Davis
>
> Liz went outside to put her toys away. It was hot. The trees did not move. No people were out. Then Liz felt water. She jumped. She ran to the house as the rain came.
>
>

 **Directions** Read "Before the Storm" with your child. Ask your child, "Who is the author of this story?" and "What is the author's reason for writing this story?"

Read the story.

The Monster
By Nate Sampson

One day, John was in the woods. He saw a big egg. He took it home. A baby monster came out! John told his mother. They put it in a basket. Soon the monster was too big for the basket. John took the baby monster back to the woods. Then it ran away.

School + Home **Directions** Read "The Monster" with your child. Ask your child, "Who is the author of the story?" and "What is the author's reason for writing this story?"

Name _____

Read the letter.

Dear Mom,

    I would like a raise. I will help clean the house more. I will walk the dog every day. I have not had a raise this year. If I got one, I would save some money too.

Love,
Kim

Name _____

Read the text and answer the questions that follow.

Wrong Feet

Jen has a brother named Sam. Sam puts on his shoes. His left shoe is on the right foot. Jen laughs. "Sam, your shoes are on the wrong feet," she says.

Sam looks at his feet. Then he smiles. "Jen, I KNOW these are my feet."

1. What is the author's purpose for writing the text?

_____

_____

_____

2. How did you decide this?

_____

_____

_____

Directions Read "Wrong Feet" with your child. Ask your child the author's reason for writing the text and write his or her response on the first line. Then have your child tell what in the text helped him or her decide the purpose. Write the response on the second line.

Name _____

Read the text and fill in the Web.

Knut, the Famous Polar Bear

Knut is a baby polar bear that was born at a zoo. He was born in 2006. When he was born, he was the size of a ball of snow.

After he was born, Knut's mother left him. A person at the zoo took care of him. Knut was the first baby polar bear to live and grow up at the zoo in many years. Today Knut is a famous polar bear.

Directions Read "Knut, the Famous Polar Bear" with your child. Ask your child about the author's purpose. Then have your child fill in the Web. Have him or her fill in the center oval with the author's purpose and topic, such as *information about Knut.* Then have your child fill in facts from the text in the outer ovals of the Web.

Name _____

Read the letter.

Dear Grandpa,

Our trip to the national park has been fun! Yesterday we hiked. The air was cool and dry. I could smell the fresh grass and flowers. We even saw a brown deer eat grass. The sun looked red and orange like a fire before it set.

Love,
Juan

Directions Read the letter with your child. Ask your child to tell the topic and the author's reason, or purpose, for writing the letter. Then have your child tell what Juan describes in the letter.

Comprehension Lesson 1   Author's Purpose **7**

Name _____

Read the story.

Closed!

  Nick went to the store to get new shoes. He wanted to get blue and white shoes. Nick pulled on the door of the store. The door did not open. Oh, no! The shoe store was closed.

Directions Read "Closed!" with your child. Ask your child, "What happens?" and "Why does it happen?"

Comprehension Lesson 2

Name _____

Read the story.

Tacos at Ann's

Rose went to Ann's house for lunch. Ann's mother made tacos. Rose was happy. Rose liked tacos a lot. Rose was very hungry. She ate three tacos! Then she was too full for cake.

School + Home **Directions** Read "Tacos at Ann's" with your child. Ask your child, "What happens?" and "Why does it happen?"

Name _____

Read the passage.

Thank You, Busy Bees

Bees are busy because they dance and make honey. Bees get food from flowers. They dance so they can tell other bees where flowers are. Then the bees make honey.

Honey tastes good, so people cook with it. They also put it on bread.

School + Home

Directions Read "Thank You, Busy Bees" with your child. Ask your child to find the cause-and-effect clue words *so* and *because*. Read those sentences together. Ask your child, "What happens?" and "Why does it happen?" in each of those sentences.

Comprehension Lesson 2

Name _____

Read the passage.

My Friends

Ben reads a lot because he likes books. He likes books about airplanes.

Sarah likes animals, so she goes to the zoo. She looks at the animals there.

Because Tina likes music, she sings and dances a lot. She sings and dances at our school.

I like books, animals, and music, too. I like my friends!

Directions Read "My Friends" with your child. Ask your child to find the cause-and-effect clue words *because* and *so*. Read those sentences together. Ask your child, "What happens?" and "Why does it happen?" in each of those sentences.

Comprehension Lesson 2   Cause and Effect **11**

Name _____

Read the story.

A Soggy Lunch

   I walked to the park to eat my lunch. The park
is far away from my house, so I was tired when I
got there. I sat down on a blanket on the grass. The
sky got dark. It started to rain, and I got wet. After it
rained, I was still hungry. I wanted to eat my lunch.
When I opened my lunch, it was wet, too! I didn't
care. I ate it anyway.

Directions Read "A Soggy Lunch" with your child. Have him or her tell you what
happens in the story and why these things happen. Ask, "What effects does the rain
cause?" Remind your child that a cause can have more than one effect.

Name _____

Read the passage.

The Stagecoach Driver

Driving a stagecoach was a hard job. A stagecoach would sometimes tip over. It rode down roads full of rocks.

Charley Parkhurst drove a stagecoach. He wore an eye patch because he could not see out of one eye. Charley worked for 20 years. When he died, people found out Charley's secret. Charley was a woman!

Charlotte Parkhurst wanted to drive a stagecoach, but only men could drive at that time. Charlotte changed her name to Charley. She put on men's clothes. For 20 years, no one knew her secret.

Directions Read "The Stagecoach Driver" with your child. Ask your child, "What happens?" and "Why does it happen?" When you read or tell your child a story, talk about what happens and why it happens.

Name _____

Read the stories.

Kim's New School

Kim likes her new school. She likes her teacher, Miss Black. Kim talks a lot. Kim is smart and funny. She likes math.

Joe's New School

Joe likes his new school. He likes his teacher, Miss Black. Joe is quiet. He does not talk a lot. He likes reading. Joe is smart.

 **Directions** Read the stories with your child. Ask your child, "How are Joe and Kim alike?" and "How are they different?"

Comprehension Lesson 3

Name _____

Read the story and fill in the chart.

The Science Report

Miss Black asks the children to write about an animal. Kim and Joe work together. Joe likes bears, but Kim does not like bears. Kim likes birds. Kim and Joe both like monkeys. Their paper is on monkeys. Joe likes to read. He reads about monkeys. Kim likes to talk. Kim talks to the class about monkeys.

Alike	Different

School + Home **Directions** Read "The Science Report" with your child. Ask your child, "How are Kim and Joe alike?" and "How are they different?" Then help your child fill in the chart.

Name _____

Read the stories.

Daytime Hiking Trip

Jack woke up early to hike in the woods. He went with his family. It was cold, so they wore coats. The sun was bright. Jack saw lots of trees. He also saw two squirrels. The squirrels played in the trees. Jack was tired when he got home. He went to sleep.

A Walk at Night

Jane and her family walked in the woods at night. They wore coats because it was cold. The woods were dark. Jane saw lots of trees. She also saw a raccoon. The raccoon hid in the leaves. Jane could not sleep when she got home.

Directions Read the stories with your child. Ask your child, "How are the hikes alike?" and "How are they different?" After your child lists each similarity or difference, have him or her point to the part of the text that helped him or her find the answer.

Comprehension Lesson 3

Name _____

Read the stories.

Fred's New Home

Dan threw a ball in the house. He broke Fred the fish's glass home. "Oh no!" yelled Dan. Fred landed on the floor. Dan quickly picked up Fred and ran to the kitchen. He put Fred in a glass of fresh water. Dan mopped up the mess. Fred was okay in the glass, but Dan knew Fred could not live in the glass forever. Dan told his father what happened.

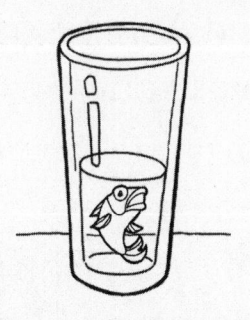

Mother's Flowers

Paul was playing ball in the house. He tripped and broke his mother's vase. The flowers fell to the floor, and water splashed. Paul ran to the kitchen. He put the flowers in a glass of water. He found a towel and cleaned up the spilled water. Then he told his mother what had happened.

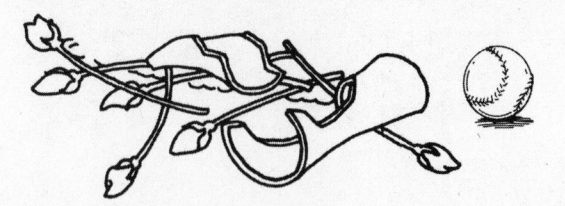

School + Home

Directions Read the stories with your child. Ask, "How are the stories about Dan and Paul alike?" and "How are they different?" After your child lists each similarity or difference, have your child point to the part of the text that helped him or her find the answer.

Name _____

Read the paragraph.

Aunt Elsa

Maria's favorite aunt was her Aunt Elsa. Like Maria, Aunt Elsa lived on Oak Street. However, Aunt Elsa lived in a small house, and Maria lived in a big house. Maria's parents worked in an office, but Aunt Elsa worked in a bakery. Maria and her family woke up at 7 a.m. every day. However, Aunt Elsa woke up at 4 a.m. Both Maria and Aunt Elsa walked home together at 3 p.m. every day.

Directions Read "Aunt Elsa" with your child. Ask your child to circle the comparison clue words and underline the contrast clue words. Then have your child use the clue words to tell what is being compared and contrasted in the paragraph.

Name _____

Read the paragraph.

Uncle Frank

Jim lived in the city. During spring break, Jim
visited his Uncle Frank. Unlike Jim, Uncle Frank lived in
a small cabin in the mountains. Like Jim, Uncle Frank
had brown hair and wore glasses. However, Uncle
Frank was taller than Jim. When they walked in the
woods, Uncle Frank and Jim both wore coats. They
took a break. Jim ate an apple, and Uncle Frank ate
two apples.

Alike	Different

Directions Read "Uncle Frank" with your child. Ask your child to circle the clue words
and list the comparisons and contrasts in the chart. After listing each similarity or
difference, have your child point to the part of the text that helped him or her find that
comparison or contrast.

Name _____

Read the passage. **Tell** the main idea.

Favorite Colors

I like the color green. Grass is green. Rob likes the color blue. The sky is blue. A lake is blue too. Joy likes the color red. Red is the color of flowers and apples. What colors do you like?

School + Home **Directions** Read "Favorite Colors" with your child. As you read the passage, discuss what the passage is mostly about. Ask your child "What is the main idea of the passage, or what is it mostly about?"

Name _____

Read the paragraph. **Tell** the main idea.

Flying a Kite

What a good day to fly a kite! My kite has four
colors. It is yellow and blue. It is red and white too.
It has a long tail. I hold my kite. Then I run. The wind
makes my kite fly. It flies high!

School + Home **Directions** Read "Flying a Kite" with your child. After you read the paragraph, have your
child tell the main idea of the paragraph, or what the paragraph is mostly about.

Name _____

Read the story. **Tell** the main idea.

Eggs and Milk

I went to the store with my dad. Mom asked us to get eggs and milk. Dad wanted to get bread. I wanted to get fruit. We looked at the toys. Then we went home. Mom asked for the eggs and milk. We forgot to buy them! We had to go back to the store.

Directions Read "Eggs and Milk" with your child. As you read the story, discuss the main idea, or what the story is mostly about.

Read the passage.

A Bright Smile

Doctor Brown takes care of my teeth. I take care of them too. I want to keep my smile bright.

I do not eat too many sweets. I eat food that is good for my teeth, such as milk.

I brush my teeth. I brush them three times a day. I want to keep my teeth clean and strong.

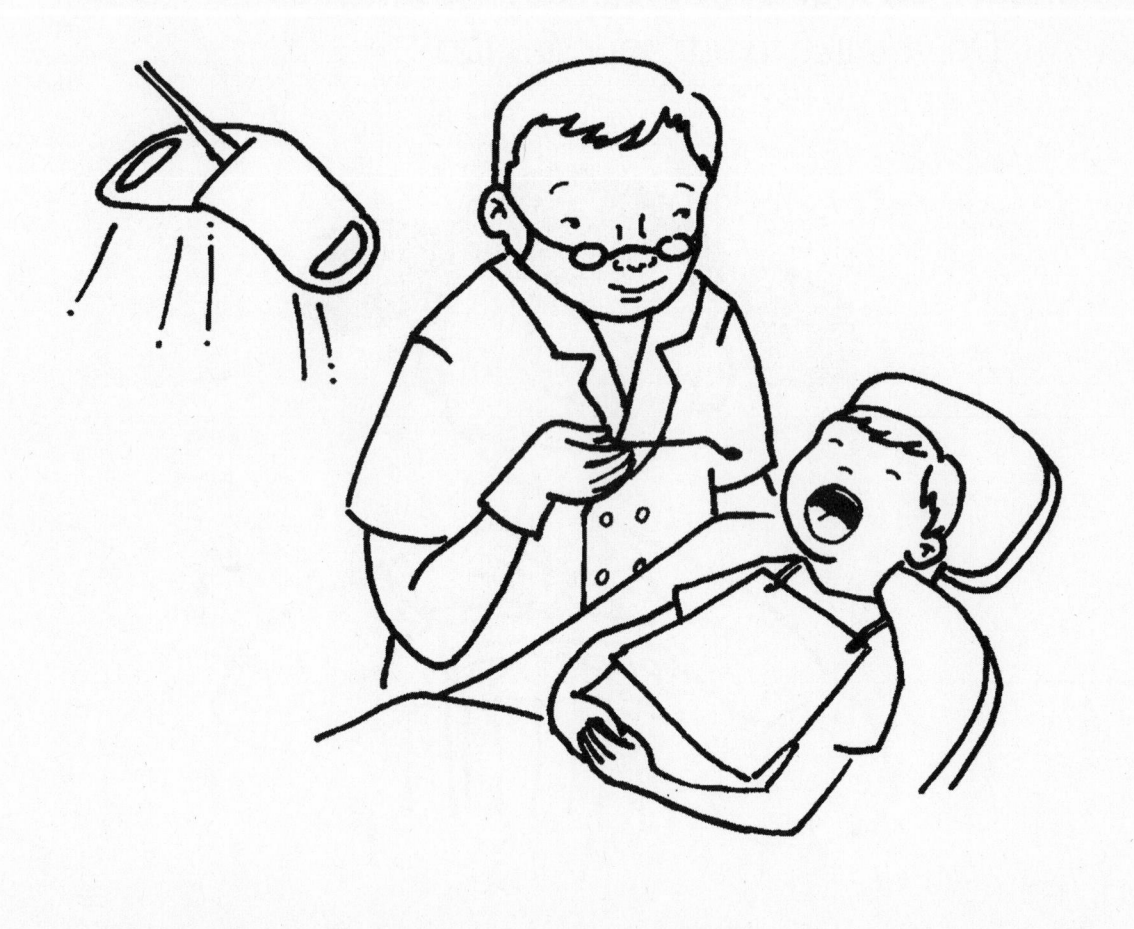

Directions Read "A Bright Smile" with your child. After you read, ask your child "What is the story's main idea, or what is it mostly about?" and "What are some details that give more information about the main idea?" Have your child circle the main idea and underline three details.

Name _____

Read the passage.

Popcorn!

I like popcorn. There are so many reasons why I like it.

The word *popcorn* is fun to say. Popcorn is fun and easy to eat. I like making popcorn at home or getting it at the movies. Popcorn is also fun to share.

Popcorn can be a good snack. You can put melted cheese on top. Or you can add peanuts to it.

Do you like to eat popcorn too?

Directions Read "Popcorn!" with your child. After you finish reading, talk about the main idea, or what the passage is mostly about. Then work with your child to identify at least three supporting details that tell about the main idea.

Name _____

Read the passage.

Giraffes

Giraffes are interesting animals. Giraffes are the tallest land animals. They have long, thin legs and long, thick necks.

Giraffes can reach leaves high in the trees. Giraffes spend most of their time eating.

A giraffe has spots on its coat. The spots help giraffes hide from their enemies.

Directions Read "Giraffes" with your child. As you read, discuss the main idea, or what the passage is mostly about. Then ask your child to identify at least three supporting details that tell about the main idea.

Comprehension Lesson 4

Main Idea and Details **25**

Name _____

Read the paragraph.

Ron and Charlie

Ron got a puppy. His name is Charlie. First, Ron plays with Charlie and takes him for a walk. Next, Ron takes pictures of Charlie. Charlie is happy. Then Ron feeds Charlie. Finally, Ron gives Charlie a bath. Now Ron and his puppy are both tired!

Directions Read "Ron and Charlie" together with your child. Ask your child, "What happens first?" "What happens next?" and "What happens after that?"

Comprehension Lesson 5

Name _____

Read the paragraph.

Eddie's Busy Evening

Eddie came home from school. He had a busy evening. First, he went to the store with his father. Next, he walked his dog. Then he helped his mother make dinner. Last, he helped clean up the table.

Directions Read "Eddie's Busy Evening" together with your child. Ask your child, "What happens first?" "What happens next?" and "What happens last?" Then have your child tell the story events in the correct sequence.

Read the story.

The Cake Mystery

Al made a cake. He put it on the table to cool.
When he came back later to eat it, the cake was gone!

First, Al asked his brother Joe. Joe did not eat it.

Next, Al asked his sister Deb. Deb did not eat it.

Last, Al looked in his room. There sat his dog,
Scraps, with cake in his mouth!

School + Home **Directions** Read "The Cake Mystery" together with your child. Ask your child to find the sequence clue words *First, Next,* and *Last.* Read those sentences together. Ask your child, "What happened?" Then have your child retell the story in the correct sequence.

Name _____

Read the paragraph.

Tadpole to Frog

A frog begins as a tiny egg. First, a mother frog lays many eggs in a pond. Next, tadpoles come out of the eggs. Tadpoles swim under water using their tails. Then each tadpole grows legs. Its tail goes away. Last, the tadpole becomes a frog.

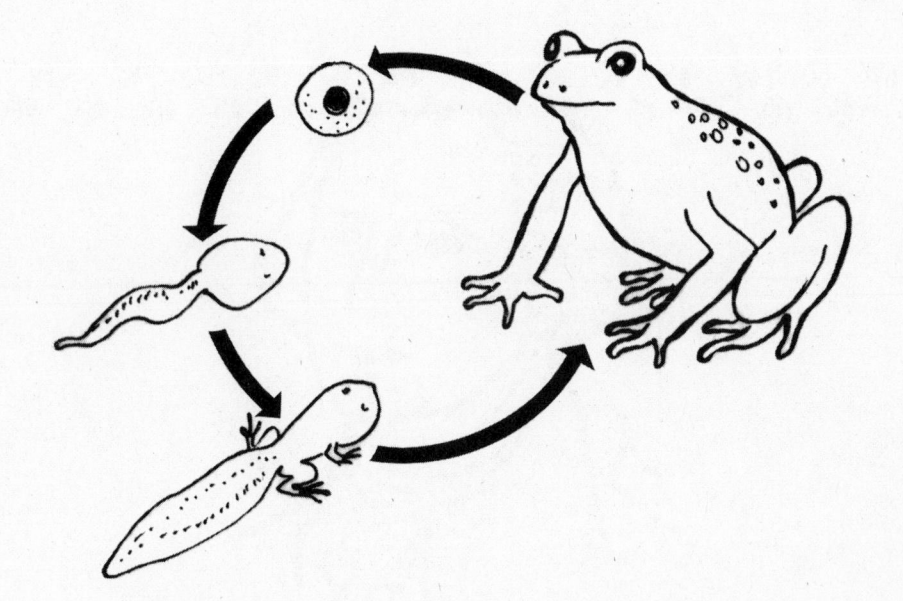

School + Home

Directions Read "Tadpole to Frog" with your child. Ask your child to circle the sequence clue words and tell you what happens first, next, and last in the paragraph. Finally, ask your child what he or she did today, using the words *first, next, then,* and *last.*

Name _____

Read the passage.

George Washington

George Washington was our first president. He was born in 1732 in Virginia. Washington fought for his country. In 1775, he became head of the army. Washington became president in 1789. Washington was president for two terms. He died in 1799.

Name _____

Read the passage.

The Pony Express

In 1860, the mail was very slow. People wanted their mail fast, so the Pony Express began.

Pony Express riders could get mail to people fast. First, one horse and rider ran about 10 miles. After that, the rider got a new horse. Then the riders got very tired. They stopped after 100 miles. Finally, a new rider would take over.

School + Home

Directions Read "The Pony Express" together with your child. Ask your child, "What happens first?" and "What happens next?" Continue until your child retells the main events in the correct order.

Name _____

Read the story.

Out of Sight

Kelly went to the sea with her family. She wanted to see the fish. She opened her eyes under water. "Ouch!" cried Kelly. The salt water hurt her eyes.

Directions Read "Out of Sight" together with your child. After reading, ask your child, "Could this story really happen?" Then ask, "How do you know?"

Name _____

Read the story.

The Short Cut

Adam left school for the day. He took a short cut home. He walked through a forest. Then he stopped to look at a rabbit. It was getting dark. Adam saw a bird in a tree. "You'd better hurry up if you want to get home before dark!" said the bird. Adam picked up his bag. He ran home.

School + Home **Directions** Read "The Short Cut" together with your child. Ask your child, "Could this story really happen, or is it make-believe?" Then ask, "How can you tell?"

Name _____

Read the story.

Alive!

Rachel loved to look for shells. Her family took
a trip to the sea. All day she walked in the sand. She
picked up every pretty shell she found. That night
Rachel put her shells on the floor. "Are all those shells
empty?" asked her mother. Rachel nodded. Then
something poked her leg. Rachel jumped. One of
the shells was a crab!

Directions Read "Alive!" together with your child. After reading, ask your child if the
story could really happen or if it is make-believe. Then ask, "How can you tell?"

Comprehension Lesson 6

Read the stories.

Catch

Billy and Chris went to the park to play catch. Billy threw the ball hard, and Chris missed it. Chris ran to look for the ball in the flowers. He could not find it. Then Chris saw something move. It was a baby rabbit! The rabbit ran away, and Chris found the ball.

Benny

The giant named Benny lived in Jack's room. Benny played with Jack's toys. He looked at Jack's baseball cards. Then he looked out the window. He saw a lady and waved. She jumped.

School + Home

Directions Read "Catch" and "Benny" together with your child. After reading each story, ask your child if it could really happen or if it is make-believe. Then ask, "How can you tell?" Have your child list two details from each story to support his or her response.

Comprehension Lesson 6   *Realism and Fantasy* **35**

Name _____

Read the story.

The Race

Hippo wanted to run as fast as Cheetah. "How could you run as fast as I?" laughed Cheetah. Hippo decided that if he wanted to run like Cheetah, he needed to look like Cheetah. So Hippo painted spots on his back.

"I'm ready," said Hippo. "Let's race." Cheetah laughed, but he agreed to race.

The race started, and Cheetah ran far ahead. Cheetah looked back at Hippo and laughed. Then Cheetah's foot fell in a hole. "Help!" cried Cheetah. Hippo was slow, but he caught up to Cheetah at last. Hippo stopped and used his teeth to dig Cheetah's foot out of the hole. Cheetah never laughed at Hippo again.

Directions Read "The Race" together with your child. Ask your child, "Is this a realistic story or a fantasy?" Then have your child list three details from the story that support his or her answer.

Read the stories.

Hannah and the Hamster

Hannah woke up sneezing. Her eyes watered. Then her brother Kurt ran into her room. "Hey, Hannah. Have you seen Nutmeg?" Nutmeg was Kurt's hamster. Hannah sneezed. Oh, no! Hamsters made her sneeze. Hannah and Kurt looked in her dresser. They looked in her shoes. Hannah's eyes watered. "I feel sick. I am going back to bed," she said. In bed, Hannah sneezed again. Kurt lifted her blanket. "There you are!" he said and picked up Nutmeg.

The Report

Joey had a report due tomorrow. He wished a tornado would come so he would not have to finish his report. Joey found a book on tornadoes. The pictures looked so real. Joey poked a page. His finger went through the book! He put his head in and then his whole body. Inside the book, the tornado chased Joey. He could not hide from the tornado. "Help! Get me out of here!" Then Joey was back at home. Writing a report did not seem so bad now!

Directions Read "Hannah and the Hamster" and "The Report" with your child. Ask your child whether each story is a realistic story or a fantasy. Then have your child list two details from each story that support his or her answer.

Read the story.

The Nest

Jen heard singing every morning. It always woke her up. Jen looked out her window. A large tree grew outside her window. There was a bird's nest in the tree.

Directions Read "The Nest" together with your child. Then ask, "What wakes Jen every morning?" and "How do you know?" Have your child use information in the story and what he or she already knows to figure out the answer to the question.

Read the story.

The Gift

Kate's grandmother was sick. Kate had a pretty picture of her grandmother with her family. She colored a box for the picture. She used colors her grandmother liked. Kate gave the gift to her grandmother. Her grandmother opened the gift. Then she smiled. She touched Kate's hand. She had tears in her eyes.

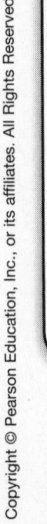

Directions Read "The Gift" together with your child. Then ask, "Does Kate's grandmother like the gift?" and "How do you know?" Have your child use information in the story and what he or she already knows to figure out the answers.

Name _____

Read the story.

The Laundry Basket

Chris had a little brother named Joey. Joey liked
to clean. Joey liked to help pick up clothes. He threw
them in the laundry basket. Sometimes he also threw
toys and other things in the basket. One day Chris lost
a book. He looked and looked for it. Then he heard a
loud bang. Just then, Chris saw Joey run away from
the basket.

What I Know	What I Read	My Conclusion

Directions Read "The Laundry Basket" together with your child. Ask, "What do you
think happened to Chris's book?" Have your child draw conclusions to answer the
question by filling in the graphic organizer. Then have your child tell you why his or
her conclusion makes sense.

Comprehension Lesson 7

Name _____

Read the story.

Karate Class

Sandy went to karate class. The children learned new moves. The teacher told Liz that she was doing well. He told Tyrone that he was doing well too. Sandy talked when the teacher was talking. The teacher asked Sandy to be quiet. That day Sandy walked home with her head down. She went to her room. Then she closed her door with a bang.

School + Home

Directions Read "Karate Class" together with your child. After reading the story, ask, "How does Sandy act after the teacher tells her to be quiet?" Then ask, "What does this tell you about how Sandy feels?" Have your child circle clues in the text and draw conclusions to figure out the answer. Have your child tell you why his or her conclusions make sense.

Name _____

Read the passage.

Giant Redwoods

Redwood trees grow in California near the ocean. They can grow to be almost 400 feet tall. Redwood trees can also grow very old. Some redwoods are 2,200 years old.

Redwoods have red and brown bark that is soft and thick. Older redwoods have thick, gray bark. This thick bark helps stop fire from burning the trees. There are no bugs that eat redwoods. People sometimes cut down redwoods for their wood.

What I Know	What I Read	My Conclusion

Directions Read "Giant Redwoods" together with your child. Ask, "What do you think causes the most problems for redwoods?" and "How can you tell?" Then have your child fill in the organizer to draw conclusions to answer the questions. Next, have your child tell why his or her conclusion makes sense.

Name _____

Read the passage.

Gold!

In 1848, people found gold in the west. The news spread fast. In 1849, people from all over traveled west. They wanted to get rich. The trip was dangerous, and it took many months.

Not everyone found gold. But many people became successful for other reasons. Some people sold tools to help people find gold. Others sold food. Some people sold places for people to live.

Directions Read "Gold!" with your child. Ask, "Who was successful during the gold rush?" and "What does this tell you about the people who came to California during the gold rush?" Have your child answer the questions and tell how the information in the passage supports his or her conclusion.

Name _____

Read the story.

The Jones Family

There are four people in the Jones family. Each person has an animal he or she likes. Father Fred likes birds best. Mother Mary likes dogs. Sister Julie likes cats most of all. Brother Bob loves pigs. Yet the Jones family only has one pet. It's a fish!

School + Home

Directions Read "The Jones Family" together with your child. Ask your child, "How many characters are there?" "What are their names?" and "What can you remember about each character?"

Name _____

Read the story.

Four Brothers

I have four brothers. My brother Ken reads a lot.
He likes school. My brother Matt has lots of friends.
He always tells jokes. My brother Alan likes animals.
My brother Tim likes to play ball. He is on a team.

Directions Read "Four Brothers" together with your child. Point to each name and ask your child, "What is the character's name?" and "What do you remember about this character?"

Name _____

Read the story.

Maria's Visit

Maria has brown eyes and long dark hair. She visited her grandfather. He has the same dark eyes as Maria. It was a warm day. Grandfather could not walk. He sat in his chair and looked out his tiny window. Maria felt bad for him. Then she had an idea. She wheeled his chair outside. Now he could see and enjoy the day too.

Directions Read "Maria's Visit" together with your child. Ask, "Which characters are in the story?" "What is Maria like?" and "What does Maria do?"

Comprehension Lesson 8

Name _____

Read the story.

After School

Josh had to watch his little brother Sam after school. One day, Josh's friend Van invited him over. Josh asked his mother if he could go. She said no. "I am sorry. I need you to watch Sam," she said. First, Josh was upset. Then Sam asked Josh to push him on the swings. Josh felt proud. He knew his family needed him.

School + Home **Directions** Read "After School" together with your child. Ask, "Which characters are in the story?" "What is Josh like?" and "What does Josh do?"

Name _____

Read the story.

Under the Bed

Todd wanted to go swimming with his friends. His dad said he had to clean his room first. Todd hated cleaning his room! He also didn't want to stay inside on a nice day.

Todd threw everything under his bed. Then he left to go swimming.

Todd's dad saw him leaving. "Wow!" he said. "You did a great job cleaning." Todd turned red, and he looked down at the floor. He felt horrible. Then he told his dad the truth.

"Well," said his dad. "You'd better finish cleaning if you want to swim today." Todd sighed and finished cleaning. Finally, he went swimming.

Directions Read "Under the Bed" with your child. Ask, "Who are the characters in the story?" and "What are they like?" Then ask, "What might be Todd's motivation, or reason, for throwing everything under the bed?" and "What might be his motivation for telling his dad the truth?"

Name _____

Read the story.

The Photos

One day Becky and Sue went to the museum. Sue liked to take pictures. She had her camera with her.

The guard inside stopped Sue. "No cameras," he said. Sue put her camera away.

At the museum the girls saw beautiful pictures of the city. "I wish I had my camera," said Sue. She wanted to remember the pictures. Then they passed the gift shop. "Wait here," said Becky. When she came back, she handed Sue a bag. Inside were cards of the pictures Sue liked best.

School + Home **Directions** Read "The Photos" together with your child. Ask, "Who are the characters?" and "What are they like?" Then ask, "What might be Becky's motivation, or reason, for buying Sue postcards?"

Name _____

Read the story.

Tomatoes

Lee wanted to grow a garden.
He asked his parents for help.
They planted a vegetable garden.
His mom planted tomatoes too.
Then they watered the plants every day.
Lee and his parents watched the plants grow.
Then they picked the tomatoes and ate them.
Lee did not like tomatoes before.
Now he does!

Directions Read "Tomatoes" with your child. Ask your child, "What is the first thing that happens?" "What happens next?" and "What happens in the end?" Have your child explain what happens in his or her own words.

Name _____

Read the story.

May and the Bee

May picked apples from the tree. She put them in a basket. Then May heard a funny sound. She saw a bee. She was scared. She ran away from the bee. Then the bee flew away. Later May started to pick apples again.

First Event

Next Event

Next Event

Last Event

School + Home **Directions** Read "May and the Bee" together with your child. Ask, "What is the first thing that happens?" "What happens next?" "What happens after that?" and "What happens in the end?" Have your child write each event in order in the organizer above.

Read the story.

Something New

Juan wanted to learn to ski, but he was afraid. He put on his skis. He went to the ski hill. But Juan could not move. He was too scared.

Juan's friend Kevin said, "We can go together. I will show you how." Kevin and Juan went down the hill together.

"That's fun!" said Juan. "I want to ski as well as you!"

School + Home

Directions Read "Something New" together with your child. Ask, "What happens in the beginning?" "What happens in the middle?" and "What happens in the end?" Check that he or she tells the events in the correct order.

Name _____

Read the story.

Amy's Bird

Amy had a pet bird. She sang to her bird. One nice day, Amy put the birdcage outside.

Then Amy's mother called her. Amy went inside. She forgot about the bird.

Amy ran outside the next morning. "Oh, no!" said Amy. Her bird was gone.

Then she looked up. Her bird was in the tree! Amy sang to her bird, and it flew to her. Amy smiled and brought it inside.

First Event

Next Event

Next Event

Last Event

Directions Read "Amy's Bird" together with your child. Ask, "What happens in the beginning?" "What happens in the middle?" and "What happens in the end?" Then have him or her record the important events in the organizer above.

Name _____

Read the story.

Lost and Found

Grandma made Val a new hat. The hat was soft. It had pink and green flowers.

Val wore her hat on the bus. She wore it in class. Then she got hot, so she put her hat in her desk.

After school, Val took the bus home. Val felt her head. Her hat was gone! Where did she leave it?

The next day Val asked the bus driver about her hat. Then she asked her teacher. No one had seen her hat. Val sighed and opened her desk. There was her hat!

First Event

Next Event

Next Event

Last Event

Directions Read "Lost and Found" together with your child. Ask, "What happens in the beginning?" "What happens in the middle?" and "What happens in the end?" Then have him or her record the events in the organizer. Ask, "Which event is the problem?" and "Which event is the solution?"

Comprehension Lesson 9

Name _____

Read the story.

Tryouts

Jon wanted to try out for the school play. Tryouts were at the school on Saturday. Jon's dad said he would drive Jon to tryouts. But Jon's dad was always busy. Jon hoped his dad would not forget.

Jon practiced his lines all week. He felt good about the tryouts.

On Saturday, Jon's dad drove to the store. Then he took books back to the library. Jon looked at his watch. It was getting late. Jon was afraid he would miss tryouts.

Finally, Jon's dad got home. Jon ran to the car and got in. They made it to the school just in time.

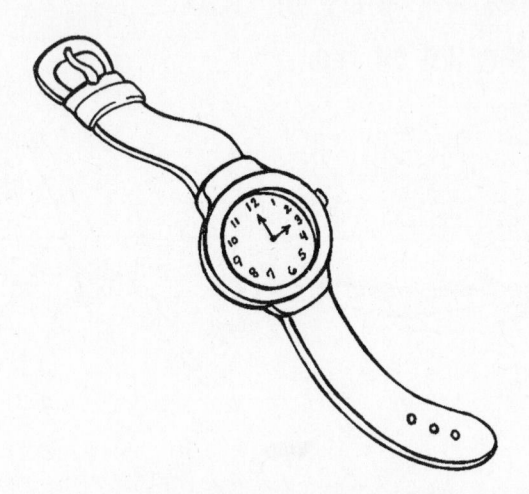

Directions Read "Tryouts" with your child. Ask, "What happens in the beginning of the story?" "What happens in the middle?" and "What happens in the end?" Then ask, "What is the problem in the story?" and "What is the solution?"

Name _____

Read the story.

The Ocean

I like the ocean.
We go there in the summer.
We stay in a red house.
We swim in the cool ocean water.
Then we look for fish.
We play in the waves.
Often we stay all day.
It is a lot of fun.

School + Home **Directions** Read "The Ocean" with your child. Ask your child, "When does this story take place?" "Where does this story take place?" and "Could the time and place be real, or is it make-believe?"

Comprehension Lesson 10

Name _____

Read the story.

Planet Zork

Last week Don moved to a new
place. It has a green sky. The water
is orange there. The trees are red
and yellow. They look like fire. Don is
the only person who lives there. Don
misses his friends. He misses his dog too.

Time	Place

Detail

Detail

Detail

Directions Read "Planet Zork" with your child. Help your child fill in the graphic
organizer. Then ask, "Could the time and place in the story be real, or is it make-
believe?" and "How do you know?"

Name _____

Read the passage.

Laura's Room

Laura is my sister. Her room is big and green. Her room has a white desk and a blue chair. She has pictures of her friends. Laura's bed is green and white. She has toys on the floor. Our cat likes to sleep in Laura's room.

Read the paragraph.

The Bottom of the Hill

There is a hill near my house. In the summer, my brothers and I play "hide and seek" there. At the top of the hill is a tree. The bottom of the hill is deep and quiet. I hide there. Then no one can find me. The wind does not touch me. The grass at the bottom of the hill is soft and green.

School + Home

Directions Read "The Bottom of the Hill" together with your child. Ask your child questions about the setting: "What is the setting?" "What is in the place?" and "What is it like?" Then have your child draw a picture of the setting in the box.

Name _____

Read the story.

Aunt Ida's

Aunt Ida lives in a tiny room above a store. The walls are all different colors. Pictures cover her walls, and books cover the floor. The sofa is covered with clothes.

Aunt Ida asked me over to help her clean. When I got there, she said, "Let's get ice cream instead." Aunt Ida loves ice cream, but she hates throwing things away.

> **Time**

> **Place**

> **Detail**

> **Detail**

> **Detail**

Directions Read "Aunt Ida's" together with your child. Help your child fill out the organizer to describe the setting. Then ask, "How is the setting related to Aunt Ida's character?" and "How might the story be different if the setting was a large, clean house with white walls?"

Name _____

Read the story.

To the Lake House

Uncle Ned and I drove up to his house by a lake. That was two years ago. We drove all afternoon through the woods. After the sun set, the air got cool. Then we heard thunder. In the black night, rain came down. We couldn't see the road. The rain poured harder and harder. Uncle Ned parked on the side of the road.

Finally, the rain stopped, and we drove ahead. Then Uncle Ned hit the brakes again. "Hold on!" he said. Two deer stood in the middle of the road. They ran across, and we drove on. We were both shaking when we got to his house by the lake.

Directions Read "To the Lake House" together with your child. Then ask, "What is the setting?" Then have your child tell you how the setting affects the plot, or the events, of the story. Finally, ask, "How might this story be different if it took place in a crowded city?"

School + Home

Name _____

Read the story.

Hot or Not?

I was inside, and I was hot. Then it started raining, so I went outside to cool off. I played and I got all wet. I was cold. Then I went back inside. I was wet, but I was not hot!

School + Home

Directions Read "Hot or Not?" together with your child. Point out the clue word *then.* Help your child pick out the key events and retell them in order, using his or her own words. *Sample answer: The girl was inside and felt hot, she went outside to play in the rain, she got wet and cold, and she went back inside.*

Comprehension Lesson 11

Name _____

Read the story.

At the Barn

Maria went to the barn. The barn was large and had many animals. She gave the horses grass. She gave them water too. Then Maria looked for eggs by the chickens. She petted the horses. Last, she left the barn and went home.

Directions Read "At the Barn" with your child. Help your child pick out the key events in the story and retell them in order, using his or her own words. Point out the clue words *then* and *last*. *Sample answer: Maria went to the barn, fed the horses, looked for eggs, petted the horses, and left.*

Name _____

Read the story.

Dinner Time

Laura wanted to cook dinner for her mother. Laura and her dad went to the store to buy everything. Then they cooked dinner. Laura set the table. Her dad put fresh flowers on the table. Dinner was ready!

Directions Read "Dinner Time" with your child. Point out the clue word *then*. Help your child pick out the key events in the story and retell them in order, using his or her own words. *Sample answer: Laura wanted to make her mother's favorite meal, Laura and her dad bought ingredients at the store, they cooked dinner, and then they set the table.*

Name _____

Read the paragraph.

Parrots

People like having parrots for many reasons. Parrots are very smart. They can learn tricks, such as "shaking hands." Some parrots can even learn to fly through hoops! Also, parrots are beautiful birds. Their feathers are bright colors, such as red, yellow, and orange. Parrots also make many sounds. They chirp and whistle. They can even learn to repeat words. People teach parrots to say "hello" or say their names.

Directions Read "Parrots" with your child. Ask, "What is the paragraph mostly about?" Help your child identify the most important idea and details in the paragraph. Ask your child to use them to summarize the paragraph in his or her own words. *Sample answer: People enjoy having parrots because they're smart, can learn tricks, are beautiful, make sounds, and can repeat words.*

Name _____

Read the story.

Cinderella

Cinderella was sad. Her sisters were mean to
her every day. One day a kind fairy gave Cinderella
a beautiful dress and shoes. Then she went to a big
party and met a prince. At 12:00, Cinderella had to
leave. She ran home and lost her shoe. The prince
found the shoe. Then the prince found Cinderella.
Now they are happy.

Directions Read "Cinderella" together with your child. Point out the clue word *then*.
Then have your child retell the key events in the story in order using his or her own
words.

Comprehension Lesson 11

Name _____

Read the paragraph.

Bicycles

Bicycles have come a long way. Early bicycles looked very different from the way they look today. In the early 1800s, bicycles were made of wood and had no pedals. Riders had to push their feet against the ground. This made them tired quickly. Riders couldn't get very far. Other bicycles had wooden wheels or wheels of two different sizes. They were very shaky to ride. They only worked well on smooth roads. Other cycles had three or four wheels instead of two. At last, pedals were added around 1860. Soon, many people in Europe and America were riding bicycles. Cycling became a new sport.

School + Home

Directions Read "Bicycles" together with your child. Ask, "What is the paragraph mostly about?" Help your child identify the most important idea and details. Then have your child use them to summarize the paragraph in his or her own words.

Name _____

Read the story.

We Wait

I wait for the bus. Joe waits for the bus. Mary waits for the bus. Dan waits for the bus. We are going to school. The bus is late. We will be late, too.

Directions Read "We Wait" together with your child. Discuss how both you and your child feel when you are late for something. Ask, "How do you think these children feel about being late for school?" As you read with your child, make connections to your own experiences.

Comprehension Lesson 12

Read the story.

Lost Kitten

Juan played by the barn. He heard a sound. Then he looked inside the barn. There was a kitten! The kitten looked sad. It was not by its mother. Juan called and found the mother cat in a basket. Then Juan put the kitten by its mother.

School + Home

Directions Read "Lost Kitten" with your child. Ask, "How do you feel when you are lost or alone?" Then ask, "How do you think this lost kitten feels at first?" and "Would you have done what Juan did?"

Read the nursery rhyme. **Then read** the story.

Hickory Dickory Dock

Hickory, dickory, dock,
The mouse ran up the clock.
The clock struck one,
The mouse ran down!
Hickory, dickory, dock.

Grandmother's Clock

Kelly stayed at her grandmother's house. One night she could not sleep. Kelly was hungry, so she went to the kitchen for something to eat. It was dark and quiet. Just then, she heard her grandmother's clock ring out. Kelly jumped! She ran back to bed.

Directions Read "Hickory Dickory Dock" and "Grandmother's Clock" with your child. Discuss how knowing the nursery rhyme can help your child understand the story. Ask, "What does the mouse do when the clock strikes?" and "What does Kelly do when the clock strikes?"

Name _____

Read the story.

On a Hot Day

It is hot today. I am eating ice cream. I must eat it
fast! Julio is drinking ice water. He must drink it fast too.
Kyle takes off his shoes. He walks on the hot path. He
must walk fast!

We are all going swimming. We wave to our
parents. The water is nice and cool. We can swim
slowly and have fun.

School + Home

Directions Read "On a Hot Day" together with your child. As you read the story,
discuss what your child already knows about hot weather. Ask such questions as, "Why
do you have to eat ice cream fast on a hot day?" and "Why do you have to walk fast
across a path on a hot day if you take off your shoes?"

Comprehension Lesson 12

Background Knowledge **71**

Name _____

Read the article.

Tulips and Daffodils

Spring is here! Birds are singing, and flowers are starting to grow. Flowers are pretty, but what if you do not have time to plant them every year?

There are some flowers that you only have to plant once. Flowers such as tulips and daffodils come up every year. Plant these flowers once, and you will have a beautiful garden each spring. Why spend time and money planting new flowers year after year when you can do it just once?

"Tulips and Daffodils" Article	What I Know About Gardening

Directions Read the first paragraph of "Tulips and Daffodils" together with your child. Discuss what your child already knows about spring flowers and gardening in general. Then read the second paragraph. Ask, "Based on what you know about gardening, why might people like to plant flowers such as tulips and daffodils?" Have your child fill in the T-Chart.

72 Background Knowledge

Comprehension Lesson 12

Read the article.

Dolphins

Dolphins are known for being friendly and playful. They like to swim with other dolphins in big groups. Some dolphins even like to swim next to ships. They leap in and out of the water. Ships create waves in the water, and dolphins like to swim in the waves.

There are many different kinds of dolphins. Some dolphins live in the ocean, and other dolphins live in rivers. Some dolphins can swim around 20 miles per hour. Most dolphins grow to about 10 feet.

Did you know that a killer whale is a type of dolphin? It's the largest kind of dolphin. Killer whales can grow to 26 feet and weigh 5 tons. They are black on top and white on the bottom. They have a white patch behind their eyes. Killer whales are smart and can be trained to do tricks.

Directions Read "Dolphins" together with your child. Discuss what your child already knows about fish and dolphins. Then ask, "How do most people feel about dolphins?" "Why do you think people were angry when they found out about the dolphins getting caught in the nets?" and "Would you have stopped eating fish if you knew it could hurt dolphins? Why?"

School + Home

Name _____

Read the story.

Ann's Birthday Party

It is Ann's birthday.
We will plan a party.
Meg will make a cake.
Lee will make a card.
Jon will bring the gift.
Here comes Ann.
She will be surprised!

Comprehension Lesson 13

Name _____

Read the passage.

In the Woods

I see a bear.
The bear is by a tree.
I see a rabbit.
The rabbit is in the plants.
I see a bird.
The bird is in a tree.
I see a squirrel.
The squirrel is on the grass.
I see other animals.
Where do you think they are?

 **Directions** Read "In the Woods" with your child. Have your child ask and answer questions about what is in the story and where things are happening.

Comprehension Lesson 13

Name _____

Read the story.

What Happened?

I reached over for an apple, but then I knocked over a glass of water. I went to get a cloth to clean it up. On my way, I tripped over the dog in the hall! I fell flat on the floor. My mother saw me. She helped me up. "How did you fall?" she asked. I told her what happened.

School + Home

Directions Read "What Happened?" with your child. Discuss what happens in the story and how it happens. Encourage your child to pause to ask and answer questions before, during, and after reading.

Name _____

Read the story.

Play Ball!

Last week, my father and I went to a ball game. We had great seats. We were in the second row, behind home plate! When the game started, I heard a man yell. He said, "Play ball!"

It was a close game. Then our team hit a home run. It was in the last inning. Dad and I had fun. I am so glad we went!

Directions Read "Play Ball!" with your child. Have your child pause while reading to ask clarifying questions, such as, "What does *inning* mean?" Also, ask your child questions about the story as you read. Have your child answer them. Encourage him or her to reread the text to find the answers.

Comprehension Lesson 13 Questioning **77**

Name _____

Read the story. **Answer** the questions about the story.

Carmen's Noisy Day

I was asleep. Then loud music woke me up. The music was coming from my brother's room down the hall. I got up and asked him to turn down the volume. He rolled his eyes, but he turned it down. Then I went back to bed.

Just then, I heard my neighbor's dog, Abby, barking. Abby was barking right outside my bedroom window! I looked out. My neighbor was throwing a stick for Abby to catch. I tried to go back to sleep, but it wasn't working. At last, I decided to get out of bed and start my noisy day.

1. When does this story take place?

2. What's the first thing that woke up Carmen?

3. Why is Abby making noise?

4. _____

Directions Read "Carmen's Noisy Day" with your child. As you read the story, ask questions that he or she can answer. Then help your child answer the three questions above. Ask your child to write his or her own question in item 4. Help your child answer the question.

Comprehension Lesson 13

Name _____

Read the story. **Answer** the questions about the story.

All in the Family

I am nine years old. I live with my mom and my grandma in an apartment. Outside my window I hear busy sounds. There are always cars, buses, and people outside. We take the bus to go places.

There is a lot of land where my aunt lives. She raises cows and chickens, and she rides horses. I cannot wait for her to visit.

My uncle lives in a cabin. When we visit him, I hear birds singing in the trees. He hikes every day. We all live in different places, but we are one big, happy family!

1. Where does the girl live?

2. Where does her aunt live?

3. Where does her uncle live?

4. _____

Directions Read "All in the Family" with your child. Ask questions for your child to think about and answer as you read the story. Focus on what is not stated directly. Encourage your child to ask and answer his or her own clarifying questions while reading. Then answer the questions above. Have your child write a question on the line and answer it.

Comprehension Lesson 13

Questioning **79**

Name _____

Read the article.

A Farmer's Job

Farmers take care of animals. Some farmers have horses and cows. Some have sheep and chickens. Farmers feed their animals. They milk the cows. They get eggs from the chickens. Farmers also need to plant food for the animals to eat. Some farmers wear hats.

Chores

1. Feed the animals.
2. Milk the cows.
3. Get the eggs.
4. Plant the corn.

Directions Read "A Farmer's Job" with your child. Have your child read the title, read the list of chores, and look at the illustration. Ask, "What do the illustration, title, and list show that might be important?" Then ask, "What are the important ideas in this passage?" Help your child find one detail that is not important in the article.

Comprehension Lesson 14

Name _____

Read the passage.

Bird Watching

Bird watching is fun. Birds are easy to watch. Many birds live in the woods or in gardens. Birds live in cities too. You can feed birds. You can listen to their songs. Books can help you learn more about the birds you see. Birds have wings. You can also have some birds as pets.

School + Home

Directions Read "Bird Watching" with your child. Have your child circle the title and repeated words in the article. Then ask, "What are some important ideas in the article?" Finally, have your child find one detail that is *not* important to the article.

Name _____

Read the article.

Hamsters Make Good Pets

Hamsters can make good pets. They are easy to care for. They are small. They also do not make much noise. Pet hamsters live in cages. Many like to play on wheels in their cages. They also like soft bedding. Many also like to play with other hamsters. Hamsters eat dried food that you can buy at the pet store. They also like seeds and fruit.

 **School + Home**

Directions Read "Hamsters Make Good Pets" with your child. Ask, "What important facts and details are in the article?" Then ask, "How do you know?"

Comprehension Lesson 14

Name _____

Read the article.

The Railroad

Many years ago people did not drive. They did not take airplanes. They walked from place to place, or they went by horse or train.

In 1869, two big train lines became one. At last, people could take one train across the country. Now people could send letters to people far away. They could see new cities and towns.

School + Home **Directions** Read "The Railroad" with your child. Ask, "What are the important ideas in the article?" Then ask, "How do you know?"

Name _____

Read the article.

Cell Phones

Cell phones are a kind of telephone. They work without a phone line or wires. Cell phones can pick up signals in the air.

People can take cell phones outside. They can use them in many places. People can use them in other countries. They can also use them in buses or on trains.

People use cell phones to do many things. The phones can get and send calls, but that is not all. Some cell phones take pictures. Others play music. Some can even connect to the Internet.

Directions Read "Cell Phones" with your child. For the first paragraph, ask, "What are the important ideas in the paragraph?" Then repeat the question for the other paragraphs.

Name _____

Read the article.

Amazing Bamboo

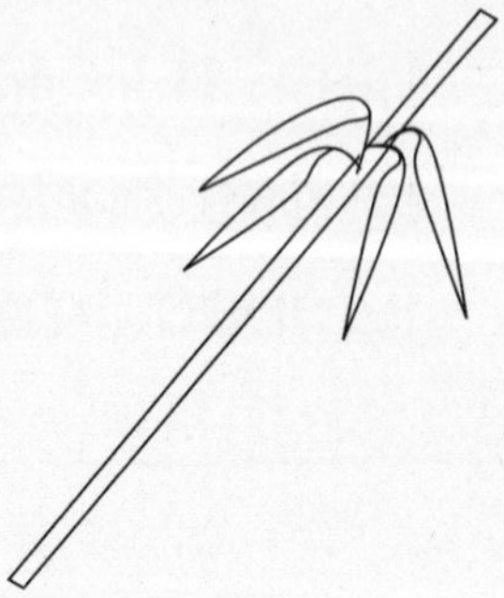

Bamboo is a strong plant that grows
quickly. Bamboo plants look like trees. Yet
they are a kind of giant grass. The plants
can grow tall very quickly. Some can grow
as high as 130 feet. They can grow
a foot each day!

Today many people have bamboo
plants in their homes and gardens. Around the world,
people use bamboo for many other things. Bamboo
is a food for people and animals. Like wood, it can be
used to make paper. It is also used to build houses,
boats, tables, floors, and clothes.

Facts and Details	Important Idea

Directions Read "Amazing Bamboo" with your child. Ask, "What are the important ideas in the first paragraph?" Then have him or her repeat the process for the second paragraph.

Comprehension Lesson 14

Important Ideas **85**

Name _____

Read the story.

Fishing Trip

Ben went fishing with his father. The lake was dark blue. It looked as flat as glass. Ben touched the water. Ducks landed. Their wings hit the water hard. Ben jumped. Then he waited for a fish to bite.

Directions Read "Fishing Trip" aloud to your child. Have your child picture the story in his or her mind. Then read it a second time together. Ask, "What from the story reminds you of what you already know about fishing?" Then have your child make a drawing in the box of what he or she pictured.

Comprehension Lesson 15

Name _____

Read the story.

First Day of School

It was the first day of school. Beth walked in the sun. She warmed her face. Her new shoes tapped on the road. Her shoes were blue and red. She smelled the grass as she walked past the lawns. She was happy to see her friends at school.

Sight	Sound	Touch

Directions Read "First Day of School" aloud to your child. Have your child picture the story in his or her mind. Then read it a second time together. Ask, "What from the story reminds you of your first day of school?" Then ask, "What did you picture in your mind as you read the story?" and "Which senses did the story make you think of?" Have your child jot responses in the chart.

Name _____

Read the first part of the story. **Then read** the second part.

Watering the Flowers

    Doug's mother asked him to watch his sister Amy. She was playing outside. Doug's mother also asked him to water the flowers by the white wood fence. Doug turned on the hose. He watered the flowers. Doug bent down to smell them. He let the water run over the white fence. Then he heard a loud scream. Doug thought Amy was hurt.

    Doug turned. Amy was fine. Just then Mrs. Brown stood up. She lived on the other side of the fence. She was all wet! Doug had watered the flowers and Mrs. Brown too! "Sorry!" said Doug.

Directions Read the first paragraph of "Watering the Flowers" and have your child visualize what is happening. Ask, "What did you picture in your mind?" Then read the second paragraph. Ask, "How did the picture in your mind change?" and "What senses did the story make you think of?" Have your child draw a picture of the second part of the story.

Comprehension Lesson 15

Name _____

Read the first part of the story. **Then read** the second part.

The Tickle

May stared at the light blue sea. The sand went on for miles. "What a beautiful place!" she thought. The trees were heavy with yellow flowers. Their leaves blew in the warm air. The white sand was fine and soft. May thought she could smell the salt from the ocean. It tickled her nose.

It was not the sea salt that tickled her nose. It was the cold winter air! Her sister had left the door open. May closed her book on beaches. Then she closed the door with a bang. "Six more long weeks of winter!" thought May.

Sight	Sound	Touch

Directions Read the first paragraph of "The Tickle" and have your child visualize what is happening. Ask, "What did you picture in your mind?" Then read the second paragraph. Ask, "How did you change the picture in your mind?" and "What senses did each part of the story make you think of?" Have your child write those details in the chart.

Comprehension Lesson 15

Name _____

Read the story.

The Garage Sale

Sara's grandfather picked up the newspaper. He looked at the small black type. "There's a garage sale down the street," he said. "Let's go take a look." Sara liked garage sales as much as her grandfather. She always found things that she had never seen before.

At the sale, Sara ran her hand across a smooth table. The table legs looked like lion feet. "We used to have one like that," said her grandfather. A box of books smelled old and damp. A bunch of glass grapes sparkled like jewels. Sara was glad she came.

Sight	Sound	Touch

Directions Read "The Garage Sale" with your child. Ask, "What did you picture in your mind as you read the story?" Have your child find at least one descriptive detail in the story for each of the five senses (see, hear, smell, touch, taste) and write them in the chart.

Comprehension Lesson 15

Name _____

Read the article.

Salt Dough Gifts

Use salt dough to make easy gifts. First, mix flour, water, and salt in a bowl. Mix the parts together until the dough is soft and stays in one piece. If it feels sticky, add more flour. If it feels dry, add more water. The dough should smell salty. Then add food coloring. (The dough is safe to eat, but it will taste salty.) Roll the dough flat and cut it into shapes. Have an adult cook the shapes on a pan in the oven for 10 minutes. Then let the dough shapes cool. Last, paint the shapes.

Sight	Sound	Touch

Directions Read "Salt Dough Gifts" with your child. Ask, "What did you picture in your mind as you read the article?" and "How did visualizing help you picture what to do for each step of the process?" Then have your child find descriptive details for three or four senses and write them in the chart.

Comprehension Lesson 15 Visualize **91**

Name _____

Cause and Effect

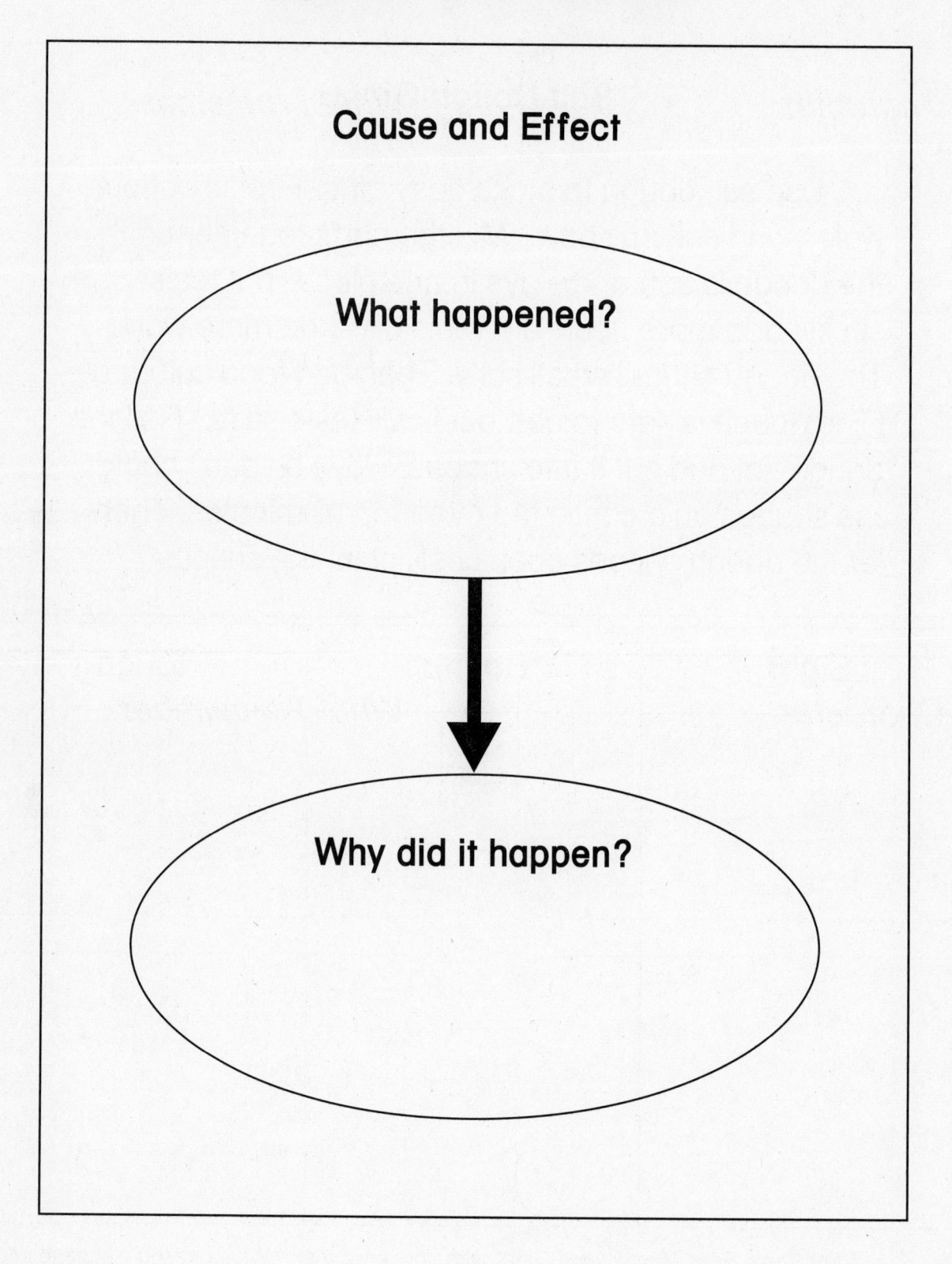

Comprehension

Name _____

Characters in a Story

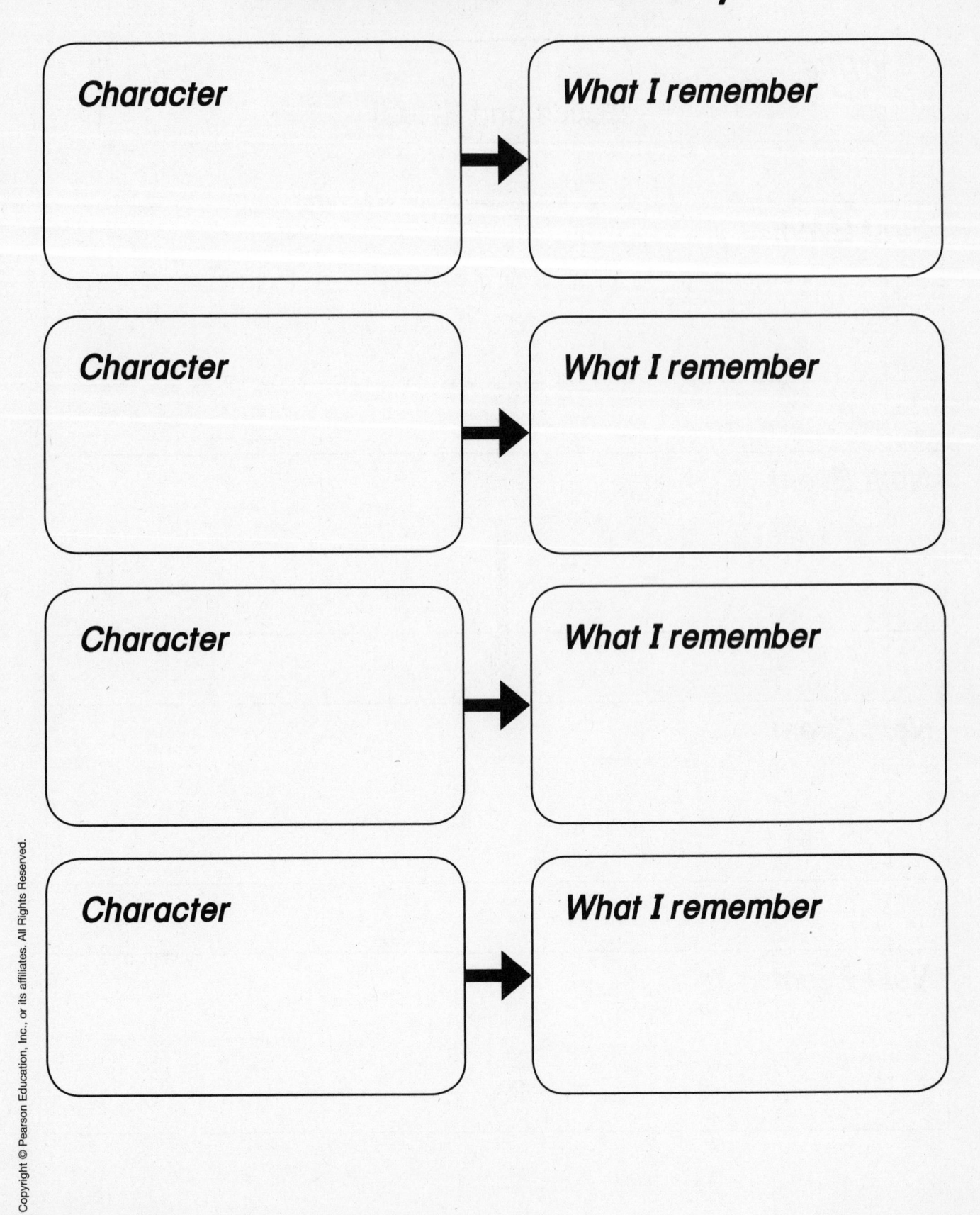

Character	What I remember
Character	What I remember
Character	What I remember
Character	What I remember

Name _____

Events in a Story

Title

First Event

Next Event

Next Event

Next Event

Five-Box Chart

3.

2.

1.

5.

4.

Name _____

Main Idea

Title: _____

Main idea: _____

_____

_____

_____

How I know: _____

_____

_____

_____

_____

_____

Comprehension

Main Idea and Supporting Details

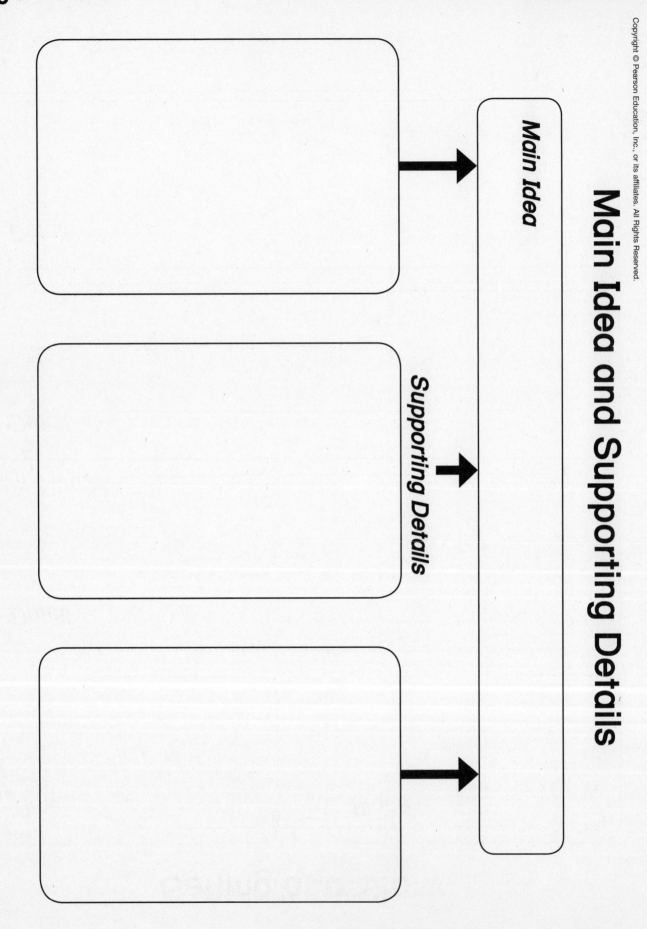

Main Idea

Supporting Details

Name

Name _____

Setting of a Story

Time

Place

Detail

Detail

Detail

Comprehension

Story Sequence B

Title	

1. First	

2. Next	

3. Then	

4. Last	

T-Chart

Comprehension

Name _____

Three-Column Chart

Web

Comprehension